How to WIN Big in U.S. Casinos and Race Tracks - non-U.S. Citizen Gamblers

It's All in the Taxes

Ω

Patrick W. Martin

Procopio International Tax Institute – San Diego, CA

First Edition – November 2013

This book is a work of non-fiction. Tax concepts, legal provisions and provisions of income tax treaties are products of governments in the U.S. and around the world. Tax concepts have no resemblance to actual persons, living or dead, events, or locales – but this really does not matter when someone is trying to understand the legal fictions created by complex U.S. tax laws!

Printed in the United States of America (or a location nearest you).

First Printing: November 2013

Procopio International Tax Institute

ISBN-978-1-49127-451-4

ACKNOWLEDGMENTS

Two of the best tax lawyers I have worked with, Eric Swenson and Jon Schimmer, have taught me an extraordinary amount about U.S. tax consequences to gamblers. They are smart and focus on their ethical obligations while advocating for clients. Many of the ideas and information, at least the good ones, in this book certainly started from their minds.

Jeff Hood is the best litigation attorney I have seen who can explain complex U.S. international tax concepts for non-resident gamblers in plain language. He can explain these concepts in tax refund suits for all to understand; for those non-resident gamblers who are fighting to get their money back.

Raymond ("Gary") Wright made this book more understandable.

Foreword

This book on international tax consequences to non-U.S. citizen gamblers addresses a very complex topic. The author's goal is to explain these complexities and their consequences in simple terms. The book tries to avoid legal citations of laws, regulations, cases and tax treaties. Inevitably, some of the most important provisions had to be cited.

Advisory

This book is intended to provide information about legal concepts to help readers understand often very complex issues within the U.S. international tax field for non-resident gamblers. Legal information is not the same as legal advice, that is, the concrete application of law to a specific case with unique and particular facts. Although the author has taken great care to make sure that the information contained herein is accurate and useful, it is always recommended to consult experienced attorneys to address any particular situation. Most importantly, if you are entitled to a large amount of taxes withheld by a Casino or Race Track, you should get advice.

TABLE OF CONTENTS

Page

TABLE OF AUTHORITIES

Page

FEDERAL CASES

FEDERAL: STATUTES, RULES, REGULATIONS, CONSTITUTIONAL PROVISIONS

CHAPTER 1
PURPOSE OF THE BOOK – KNOWING HOW TO REALLY WIN

The cover of this book is not serious. It's humorous. This book, however, is dead serious about the importance of collecting money that is owed to you; or to never allow the Casinos or Race Tracks to take it from you in the first place if you live in one of the following countries: Austria, Belgium, Bulgaria, Czech Republic, Denmark, Finland, France, Germany, Hungary, Iceland, Ireland, Italy, Japan, Latvia, Lithuania, Luxembourg, Netherlands, Russia, Slovak Republic, Slovenia, South Africa, Spain, Sweden, Tunisia, Turkey, Ukraine, and the United Kingdom.

If you are a Canadian resident, there is even a more unique and special rule applicable to you as a non-resident gambler. You will not be able to avoid the withholding tax at the Casino or Race Track, but there is a procedure under the Canadian - United States Income Tax Treaty that allows recovery of the tax withheld, explained later in the book.

These countries all have an income tax treaty with the U.S. which can mean you might owe no U.S. taxes from your gambling activities. In addition, Malta is also a country with an income tax treaty, but which has a special set of rules regarding the amount of tax imposed. If you do not live in one of these countries, your route may be much more complex. The goal in each case is to hit the jackpot of U.S. federal withholding taxes.

This book will demonstrate that the true economic rewards are not to be found in how the Casinos and Race Tracks operate or the percentage payouts in their games of chance. The real economic windfall and the way to win big is knowing how the complex U.S. tax system applies (many would say unfairly applied by the U.S. federal tax collection agency, the Internal Revenue Service – "IRS") to non-U.S. citizen non-resident gamblers.

This book identifies why the single most important aspect for a non-U.S. citizen gambler will almost always be the taxes. You might think that winning big at the game of chance played at a U.S. Casino or U.S. Race Track, is what is important. This book will demonstrate that the true economic rewards are not to be found in how the Casinos and Race Tracks operate or the percentage payouts in their games of chance. The real economic windfall and the way to win big is knowing how the complex U.S. tax system applies (many would say unfairly applied by the U.S. federal tax collection agency, the Internal Revenue Service – "IRS") to non-U.S. citizen non-resident gamblers.

It's no fun as a gambler to have the IRS take taxes that are not owing, especially after a bad night of gambling. As Judge Kavanaugh of the U.S. Court of Appeals for the District of Columbia Circuit said in the *Sang Park*[1] case:

> ***KAVANAUGH, Circuit Judge: After a night of gambling, it's no fun to walk out of the Casino a loser. But it's even worse when the IRS, on your way out, tries to tax you on each individual bet that you happened to win over the course of your losing night. Enter Sang Park, a South Korean businessman who gambled away thousands of dollars at slot machines on Casino outings during his trips to the United States – only then to have the IRS seek more in taxes.***

You are thinking to yourself "Taxes – Why do I care about taxes? I want to just win big at the Casino or the Race Track!" You should care dearly, since as a non-U.S. citizen gambler who does not reside in the U.S., you will be taxed very differently than a U.S. tax resident.

This book will more than pay for itself; hopefully at least ten-fold, a hundred fold or several thousand-fold.

The answer to the question of why you should care about taxes is simple. If you, as a non-U.S. citizen, win a single jackpot, race, or other defined game of chance of US$1,200 or more, the IRS will make sure the Casino or Race Track

[1] *Park v. C.I.R.*, 722 F.3d 384 (D.C. Cir. 2013)

withholds thirty percent (30%) of each winning gross amount of US$1,200 or more you are given. Once you learn the law, and how you can recover these withheld taxes, this book will more than pay for itself; hopefully at least ten-fold, a hundred fold or several thousand-fold. The information should enable you to break the complicated "U.S. tax code" to understand how you can recover some or the entire 30% amount of each jackpot or race you have won, or will win.

A. How to Win Big in the Game of Taxes

Not everyone can be lucky at games of chance in the Casinos or the Race Tracks in the U.S. There are, of course Casinos throughout the U.S. Some of the most famous are located in Las Vegas, Nevada; Atlantic City, New Jersey; Biloxi, Mississippi; not to mention hundreds (500+/-) of Casinos spread throughout the United States that are operated on Indian Reservations – from California, to Alaska, Texas, Florida, New York, Montana and about all other states in between. Some of the most exciting betting Race Tracks in the U.S. are found in California, Kentucky and New York, plus many other points around the country.

Much of the enjoyment of gambling can be taken away by how the Internal Revenue Service administers this 30% withholding tax, forcing the Casinos and Race Tracks to withhold on only certain winnings, without any offset for the amounts invested or wagered.

Judge Kavanaugh in the *Sang Park* case, eloquently and simply explained how the IRS applies (misapplies the law in the case of Mr. Sang Park from South Korea) the rules as follows:

> ***A simple hypothetical illustrates how U.S. citizens and non-resident aliens are taxed differently with respect to gambling winnings: Consider two people. The first, a U.S. citizen, walks into a Casino and sits down to play slots. The player first wins $100 but then loses the $100 before leaving the Casino for the night. In that hypothetical, the U.S. citizen would have $0 in income to report because the IRS interprets the applicable provision of the Tax Code to cover only gains measured over a session of gambling. The second person, a non-resident alien, also wins $100 and then loses $100. The non-resident alien is in the same financial situation as our U.S. friend. But according to the IRS, the non-resident alien has $100 in income to report (the $100 he won in the initial bet) because the IRS interprets the applicable provision to require non-resident aliens to pay taxes on gains from each bet.***

This 30%, of course, is the amount of withheld tax that is paid over by the Casino or Race Track directly to the U.S. federal government.

This book will explain that the real winnings for non-U.S. citizen gamblers "**are all in the taxes**." This is because of the rather bizarre approach taken by the U.S. Internal Revenue Service as it selectively imposes U.S. withholding taxes at source against the non-U.S. citizen gambler who is not a resident of the United States. These selectively applied rules are explained throughout the book. In short, the Casinos and Race Tracks withhold a 30% gross amount on certain winnings of non-U.S. citizen gamblers. The 30% gross withholding is made on each

This is the central point of this book. How you can recover what is legally owed to you!

"per spin" or "per bet" play that generates a winning amount of US$1,200 or more. The method by which this 30% withholding tax is imposed by the IRS, forces Casinos to withhold in all such circumstances; even if the gambler has no "income, gains or profit" at the end of their gambling sessions. This 30% withholding tax is then paid over directly by the Casino or Race Track to the IRS. Typically (if not almost always) the non-U.S. citizen gambler has a legal claim to those funds.

This is the central point of this book. How you can recover what is legally owed to you!

B. A Detailed Explanation of How the Internal Revenue Service Administers the Law is Provided Throughout This Book Which Provides You the Non-resident Gambler a Legal Right for Recovery of Taxes

The non-resident gambler can legally bring a suit against the Internal Revenue Service to recover some or all of this 30% withholding tax paid by the Casino or Race Track.

The principles of how the IRS administers the law are demonstrated below in the simple example of a US$1,200 jackpot.

Jackpot		**$1,200**
U.S. Federal Withholding Tax Rate	**30%**	
U.S. Federal Withholding Tax @ 30%		**($360)**
Amount Payable by the Casino to the IRS	**$360**	
Balance to Gambler		**$840**

If you win US$120,000 of jackpots, or more, obviously, the importance of understanding the contents of this book is even more significant for you. If you are a winner of US$120,000 of jackpots, for instance, you might be entitled to a federal income tax refund of US$36,000. That is a real jackpot! Of course, as the numbers go up, the tax refund similarly goes up and hence the economic benefit to you as the gambler. If the winnings are US$1.2M, then the tax refund is likely to be in the range of US$360,000. This represents 30% of the gross jackpot won to begin with.

That is why, the author of this book emphasizes that "***It's All in the Taxes!***"

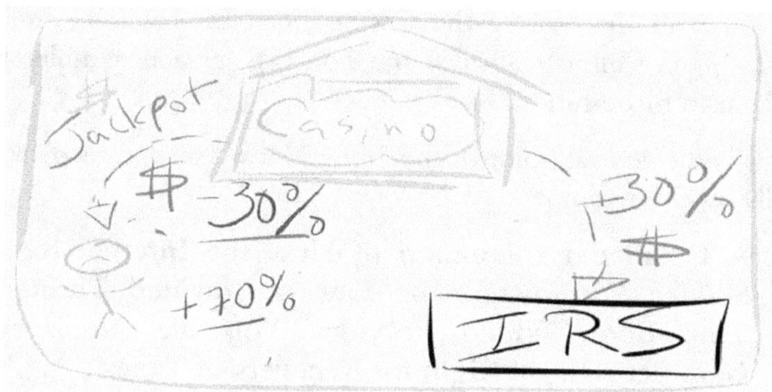

The following US$1.2M jackpot example shows how the IRS will collect US$360,000 even if they are not ultimately entitled to that amount under the law:

Jackpot		**$1,200,000**
U.S. Federal Withholding Tax Rate	**30%**	
U.S. Federal Withholding Tax @ 30%		($ 360,000)
Amount Payable by the Casino to the IRS	**$360,000**	
Balance to Gambler		$ 840,000

A net US$840,000 is a nice pay day, but if you are entitled to a tax refund of some or all of the US$360,000, the payday is obviously much better. What's more shocking, is the arbitrary amount of US$1,200 used by the IRS to require withholding by Casinos. There is a dirty little secret that no one in the government wants to explain. This "magical amount" of $1,200 does not exist anywhere in the federal tax law. The IRS simply published the $1,200 alongside the $1,200 amount required for tax reporting for U.S. citizen and U.S.

resident gamblers. The US$1,200 amount for U.S. tax resident gamblers is in the law (the regulations),[2] but the same amount used by the IRS for non-resident gamblers is NOT in the law.

C. How Non-U.S. Citizen Gamblers in U.S. Casinos and Race Tracks Can All Be Winners When It Comes to U.S. Taxes

The remainder of this book reviews key details about withholding taxes, how they are collected, what information Casinos and Race Tracks use with their non-U.S. citizen clientele, the law that applies and what steps these gamblers can take to recover money directly from the U.S. Treasury. Importantly, the law imposes some strict time limits and requires the non-U.S. citizen gamblers take specific legal steps to protect their economic rights and rights to refunds of taxes. A portion of an entire chapter (see, **CHAPTER 10** - How to Be Prepared to Go Up Against Goliath) is dedicated to these important time lines set forth in the law.

D. Taxes is Where the Big Money is . . .

It is worth repeating that "***It's All in the Taxes***!" No matter how much you as a non-U.S. citizen gambler win, knowing (i) you may be able to recover most (if not all) of the 30% withholding taxes withheld by the Casino, and (ii) the basic steps needed to take to protect your economic rights, should be invaluable to you and every other non-resident gambler. Whether your trips to the U.S. Casinos and Race Tracks start from Mexico, Brazil, South Korea, France, the United Kingdom, Kuwait, Canada, South Africa, Saudi Arabia, Hong Kong, Colombia, Germany, China, Argentina, Bahrain, or any other country around the world, a basic understanding of how the U.S. tax law works is essential for your economic success.

Casinos and Race Tracks are in the business to make money. If they did not make profit, they could not continue to operate over a

---

[2] See, Treas. Reg. Section 7.6041-1, **Return of information as to payments of winnings from bingo, keno and slot machines**, which only applies to payments made by Casinos to U.S. residents of " . . . US$1,200 or more from a bingo game or slot machine play." Those regulations relate to the reporting requirements that came into effect in the 1970s, but have no application to non-resident gamblers.

long period of time. Accordingly, the entire pool of clientele of a Casino, over the long-run, must necessarily lose to the Casino. This is, of course, what is often referred to as the "House Edge". Some gamblers win at any given time and some gamblers lose. The Casinos and Race Tracks obviously hope there are more losing than winning.

This does not mean, of course, that you cannot win; and even win big at any given time or at any given gambling session. However, no matter how big you win (or lose), as a non-U.S. citizen, you should be able to win even more knowing how to recover some or all of the monies paid by the Casinos and Race Tracks to the U.S. federal government. If you gamble and have a losing session, the withholding tax law, as administered by the IRS, still provides for taxes to be withheld from your jackpots and winnings.

E. This Book Explains the Complex U.S. Laws, Regulations, Procedures and IRS Practices in Simple Layman Terms

This book does explain the "nitty-gritty" of how the U.S. federal tax law works for non-U.S. citizen gamblers. It explains the flow of funds, the IRS forms that are used, the key considerations that any gambler should know, if they want to get back the edge from the house.

One of the challenges of the subject matter is that the law is at times mind-bogglingly complex. Attempting to explain these complex rules; to distill them to understandable concepts, is the very goal of the author. Although you may never become an expert of the U.S. international tax law and its application to the gaming industry, you should finish this book with a basic understanding of the principles most important for your gambling endeavors. The goal is to help you keep as much of your gambling winnings as possible (and recover taxes owed to you) and minimize your losses with taxes paid back to you.

F. Not A Book About Gaming or Gambling Strategies

This book does not talk about gaming strategies; how to increase your odds of winning jackpots or any other games of chance. It does not try to explain any mathematical or other quantitative methods that could improve your chances in whatever game of chance you play at any U.S. Casino. It does not purport to explain which games of chance will provide you better odds; increase your chances of minimizing losses, or other general economic notions directly stemming from the games at U.S. Casinos and Race Tracks.

No matter how much you as a non-U.S. citizen gambler win, knowing (i) you may be able to recover most (if not all) of the 30% withholding taxes withheld by the Casino or Race Track, and (ii) the basic steps needed to take to protect your economic rights, should be invaluable to you and every other non-resident gambler.

This book does explain the "nitty-gritty" of how the U.S. federal tax law works for non-U.S. citizen gamblers. It explains the flow of funds, the IRS forms that are used, the key considerations that any gambler should know, if they want to get back the edge from the House; the IRS House. This book does explain the most important economic notions of taxes and how to recover those taxes, under the law.

CHAPTER 2
ABOUT THE AUTHOR -U.S. INTERNATIONAL TAX ATTORNEY

Patrick W. Martin is the leader of the Tax Team of the California based law firm, Procopio, Cory Hargreaves & Savitch LLP ("Procopio"). His practice emphasizes international tax planning and related international law matters. He represents foreign individuals, multi-national families, companies, international athletes, entertainers, and entertainment groups in such areas as developing worldwide investment and financing structures, international tax treaty planning strategies, planning worldwide income, and estate and inheritance taxes. He helps resolve international tax controversies and develops international wealth preservation structures to complement the client's international investments and business transactions.

A. Represented Multiple Non-U.S. Citizen Gamblers in Tax Claims Against the U.S. Government

The author's law firm has extensive experience in representing gamblers in tax cases against the Internal Revenue Service with unique success. Procopio's tax lawyers, many who specialize in international tax matters, have represented numerous gamblers, both (1) non-U.S. Citizens non-resident gamblers and (2) US resident gamblers. The range of cases handled by the team of tax lawyers start with the commencement of audits by the Internal Revenue Service, through administrative appeals, through U.S. Tax Court petitions and full trials, plus multimillion dollar suits for tax refunds in the U.S. Court of Federal Claims.

B. Law Firm Practice - Advise Numerous Gamblers (Both Casual and Those Dedicated to a Trade or Business of Gambling)

The author's US-based law firm has represented numerous gamblers who are not United States citizens and were not residents in claims against the Internal Revenue Service. The tax team practice also advises US resident gamblers in specialized cases. One of the most important United States Tax Court cases was represented by Mr. Eric D. Swenson of the tax team in *Gagliardi vs. Commissioner.* http://www.procopio.com/userfiles/file/assets/files1/swenson-bio-2013-281.pdf

There are few expert lawyers who specialize in international tax law with extensive knowledge of the withholding tax for gamblers. The author represents many of these gamblers without cost to the gambler. The fees to the international tax attorney are simply deducted from any successful recovery of taxes from the Internal Revenue Service.

The law firm of Procopio, Cory, Hargreaves & Savitch, LLP has extensive experience in representing gamblers in tax cases against the Internal Revenue Service with unique success. It has represented numerous gamblers, both (1) non-U.S. Citizens non-resident gamblers and (2) US resident gamblers. The range of cases handled by the team of tax lawyers include from the commencement of audits by the IRS, through administrative appeals, through U.S. Tax Court petitions and full trials, plus multimillion dollar suits for tax refunds in the U.S. Court of Federal Claims.

CHAPTER 3
U.S. TAX WITHHOLDING REGIME – BASIC OVERVIEW

As explained, there is a 30% U.S. withholding tax imposed on certain gambling winnings at its source, i.e., at the U.S. Casinos and Race Tracks.

The basic principle is that a non-resident alien is subject to a 30% withholding tax on their "... periodical gains, profits, and income."[3] This seems clear enough and comes straight from the statute.

This amount of tax is treated by the Internal Revenue Service as the final tax owing. This however, is not the law.

Conceptually, it sounds fairly simple, but the way it has been administered by the IRS has caused much confusion. The view of the author is that the 30% withholding tax imposed by the IRS against Casinos and Race Tracks is inconsistent with the law. The IRS has construed "... periodical gains, profits, and income ... " to mean something entirely different than the plain reading of the statute. The government has required that the U.S. Casinos and Race Tracks withhold on the amount of each of your winnings that is US$1,200 or more (i.e., each "spin" or "play" that generates such a win). This 30% withholding tax of each jackpot or amount is then paid over directly to the IRS. This leaves you with only 70% of that particular jackpot or winning amount.

There are no withholding taxes on winnings from:

1. **Blackjack**
2. **Baccarat**
3. **Craps**
4. **Roulette**
5. **Bix-6 wheel**

A. Why the IRS Has the "House Edge"?

Non-U.S. citizen gamblers are always at a disadvantage compared to the U.S. federal government. There are several reasons for this "house edge" in favor of the IRS.

[3] See, Internal Revenue Code ("IRC") Section 871(a)(1)(A).

First, <u>who</u> can reasonably be expected to understand the complexities of U.S. federal tax law? The federal tax law is complicated and the withholding tax rules of Chapter 3 of Subtitle A of Title 26 (aka the "Internal Revenue Code" or "IRC") are particularly complex to understand. In addition to Chapter 3 of the IRC, there are other Subtitles (e.g., Subtitle F), numerous other Chapters of the IRC relevant to non-U.S. citizen gamblers. In addition, there are literally thousands of pages of case law applicable to gamblers, plus hundreds (if not thousands) of pages of tax regulations that impact the tax treatment of gamblers. Throw dozens of pages of the IRS Internal Revenue Manual into the mix; along with what this author views to be an incoherent policy of the IRS in its administration of withholding taxes against non U.S. citizens, and one can quickly learn that the complexity of the tax law favors the "House"- i.e., the IRS.

The Casino will immediately take the following steps when a non-U.S. citizen gambler hits a winning jackpot, race winning or other defined amount of at least US$1,200. First, they will stop play (the slot machine will physically lock up, preventing the gambler from continuing to place bets). Second, the Casino will require the gambler to provide them his or her name, address and taxpayer identification number ("TIN"). Normally the non-U.S. citizen will not have a U.S. TIN, unless and until they file a U.S. federal income tax return. The Casino will ask the gambler for identification (typically two types of verification); e.g., a passport and driver's license or voting card. From this information collected, the Casino will then prepare the correct tax forms they are required to file with the IRS.

Second, in addition to complexity, the way the law is administered necessarily favors the IRS, since Casinos and Race Tracks will always withhold the 30% tax, so as not to become liable themselves for any tax. Casinos and Race Tracks like their clientele, but like themselves even better. The U.S. Treasury wishes it to be that way; and hence the rules were drafted to essentially force Casinos and Race Tracks (or any other U.S. payors of U.S. source income) to withhold the 30% federal withholding tax, so they themselves do not become liable directly to the IRS. The law provides Casinos and Race Tracks with indemnity vis-à-vis their clients for withholding and paying the 30% tax to the IRS. If tax is not owed, the Casinos still are generally not liable to the gambler for paying it to the IRS.

This amount of tax is treated by the Internal Revenue Service as the final tax owing. This however, is not the law.

This leaves you as a non-resident gambler as the one who has to battle it out directly with the Internal Revenue Service, typically to bring a suit to recover taxes owed to you. The Casinos and Race Tracks get to "wash their hands" under the law and take no responsibility while the onus is left on your shoulders to recover the taxes owed to you under the law.

Third, there is the "dirty little secret" that no one in the government wants to explain. This "magical amount" of $1,200 does not exist anywhere in the federal tax law. The IRS simply published the $1,200 alongside the $1,200 amount required for tax reporting for U.S. citizen and U.S. resident gamblers. The US $1,200 amount for U.S. tax resident gamblers is in the law (the regulations), but the same amount used by the IRS for non-resident gamblers is NOT in the law.

Fourth, few non-U.S. citizen gamblers have any basic understanding of how the U.S. tax law works in this highly specialized area of the law. Lack of knowledge gives "the House"- i.e., the IRS, yet another edge. The lack of knowledge is only compounded, as the IRS sometimes makes up the rules as they go along in this area of non-resident gamblers.

Fifth, non-U.S. gamblers must typically hire U.S. tax lawyers to advise them and to bring a tax refund suit against the IRS. This can be expensive for the gambler if the wrong lawyer is chosen.

Sixth, language is often a barrier. The tax laws, as confusing as they are, are only in English; not Spanish, Korean, Portuguese, French, Arabic Mandarin, Dutch, or any other languages.

The chapters in this book will better explain how these taxes work and how non-U.S. citizen gamblers can recover most, if not all, of them. The goal of this book is to help reduce "the House" edge, currently held by the IRS for the non-U.S. citizen gambler.

There is a "dirty little secret" that no one in the government wants to explain. This "magical amount" of $1,200 does not exist anywhere in the federal tax law.

B. When Withholding Tax Applies – the IRS' Dirty Little Secret

The IRS requires the Casino to generally withhold 30% of any jackpot or Race Track winning of US$1,200 or more.

As previously explained, that $1,200 amount does not exist anywhere in the federal tax law. The IRS simply published the $1,200 consistent with the $1,200 amount required for tax reporting for U.S. citizen and U.S. resident gamblers. The US$1,200 amount for U.S. tax resident gamblers is in the law (the regulations), but the same amount used by the IRS for non-resident gamblers is nowhere to be found in the law. The amount does not exist in the statute or law and is just an administrative rule created by the Internal Revenue Service without any regulatory authority.

This 30% withholding tax amount is not reduced by the amounts of the wagering transaction; per the method by which the IRS administers this tax. For instance, if you bet $500 and win a jackpot or race that pays at least US$1,200, the IRS does not allow the Casino or Race Track to count your wager amount of $500 when it calculates the 30% withholding tax. The Casino or Race Track withholds 30% or US$360 in this case, even though you had to place a bet of US$500 before you could win the US$1,200 jackpot or the race. Obviously, in this simple example your bet cost you US$500, which means that economically (analyzing only this single transaction), you could never have won $1,200, but rather your gross earning amount on that particular play would have only been US$700 (i.e., US$1,200 winnings paid, reduced by the US$500 for the bet placed).

You may be asking yourself: How can 30% gross withholding tax apply on a single jackpot, when during the gambling session I had no economic gains? I left the Casino without money in my pocket.

In addition, the IRS does not allow the Casino to take into account other winnings and losses from other wagering transactions during the session.

The following numerical calculations demonstrate the results of the withholding tax withheld, and how this single transaction produces an effective tax rate of 51%:

Wager No. 1		
Jackpot or Race Winning Amount		$1,200
AMOUNT WAGERED		$(500)
"Profit" from Wager Transaction		$700
U.S. Federal Withholding Tax Rate (30%)	30%	
U.S. Federal Withholding Tax (Paid by Casino or Race Track to IRS)	30% of $1,200	($360)
Balance to Gambler	$1,200 Win Amount, Less $360 Taxes	$860
"Profit" from Wager Transaction after Taxes Paid	$1,200 Win Amount, Less $500 Amount Wagered, Less $360 Taxes	$340
Effective Tax Rate on Profit from Wager Transaction	$700 "Profit" Relative to $360 of Taxes Withheld	51%

The Casino will immediately take the following steps when a non-U.S. citizen gambler hits a winning jackpot, race winning or other defined amount of at least US$1,200. First, they will stop play (the slot machine will physically lock up, preventing the gambler from continuing to place bets).

Second, the Casino will require the gambler to provide them his or her name, address and taxpayer identification number ("TIN"). Normally the non-U.S. citizen will not have a U.S. TIN, unless and until they file a U.S. federal income tax return. See **CHAPTER 9B.iii** - U.S. Individual Taxpayer Identification Number ("ITIN") – the "Catch 22". The Casino will ask the gambler for identification (typically two types of verification); e.g., a passport and driver's license or voting card. From this information collected, the Casino will then prepare the correct tax forms they are required to file with the IRS.

What games of chance can I play at the Casino where taxes are not required to be withheld at the Casino?

The Casino will file Internal Revenue Service Form 1042-S directly with the Internal Revenue Service. That form is completed for each jackpot or winning amounts of at least $1,200 - or greater. The withholding taxes paid by the Casino will be paid over along with this particular form 1040-S.

See special rules for:

- Blackjack
- Baccarat
- Craps
- Roulette
- Bix-6 wheel

See a sample below of what is included on this form:

Form **1042-S**

Department of the Treasury
Internal Revenue Service

Foreign Person's U.S. Source Income Subject to Withholding **2013**

▶ Information about Form 1042-S and its separate instructions is at www.irs.gov/form1042.

☐ **AMENDED** ☐ **PRO-RATA BASIS REPORTING**

OMB No. 1545-0096

Copy B
for Recipient

1 Income code	2 Gross income	3 Withholding allowances	4 Net income	5 Tax rate .	7 Federal tax withheld
				6 Exemption code	8 Withholding by other agents
					9 Total withholding credit

10 Amount repaid to recipient	14 Recipient's U.S. TIN, if any ▶ ☐ SSN or ITIN ☐ EIN ☐ QI-EIN
11 Withholding agent's EIN ▶ ☐ EIN ☐ QI-EIN	15 Recipient's foreign tax identifying number, if any / 16 Country code
12a WITHHOLDING AGENT'S name	17 NQI's/FLOW-THROUGH ENTITY'S name / 18 Country code
12b Address (number and street)	19a NQI's/Entity's address (number and street)
12c Additional address line (room or suite no.)	19b Additional address line (room or suite no.)
12d City or town, province or state, country, ZIP or foreign postal code	19c City or town, province or state, country, ZIP or foreign postal code
13a RECIPIENT'S name / 13b Recipient code	20 NQI's/Entity's U.S. TIN, if any ▶
13c Address (number and street)	21 PAYER'S name and TIN (if different from withholding agent's)
13d Additional address line (room or suite no.)	22 Recipient account number (optional)
13e City or town, province or state, country, ZIP or foreign postal code	23 State income tax withheld / 24 Payer's state tax no. / 25 Name of state

For Privacy Act and Paperwork Reduction Act Notice, see instructions. Cat. No. 11386R Form **1042-S** (2013)

Notice, there is a line for a United States taxpayer identification number to be included (see line number 14). This is very important, so that the taxes withheld by the Casino or Race Track can be traced back directly to you as the particular non-resident gambler. If you do not have a United States taxpayer identification number, it will be difficult, some would say impossible, for you to be able to prove the amount of withholding taxes paid over by the Casino or Race Track on your behalf.

In all cases, it is crucial that you request and maintain in your records all copies of Internal Revenue Service Forms 1042-S. You will need to assure that the information has been accurately and completely filled out on each form 1042-S by the Casino or Race Track. See for instance, your complete and accurate address information on line 13a, 13b, 13c, etc. If you do not have correct and accurate information, it will be very difficult to successfully bring a refund action against the government to recover your taxes that are rightfully yours.

In all cases, it is crucial that you request and maintain in your records all copies of Internal Revenue Service Forms 1042-S. You will need to assure that the information has been accurately and completely filled out on each form 1042-S by the Casino or Race Track.

C. When Withholding Tax Does Not Apply

You might be interested to know that U.S. citizens and U.S. residents are never subject to the 30% withholding tax at the source.[4] Since this book is not for U.S. residents, but rather non-U.S. citizens who do not reside in the U.S., the question is: "**What games of chance can I play at the Casino and not have to have taxes withheld at the Casino?**" Fortunately, for you, the statute expressly excludes any withholding tax on the proceeds from a wager placed on any of the following games by a non-resident gambler:

- Blackjack

[4] U.S. citizens and residents are subject to special reporting by Casinos of certain gambling earnings at US$1,200 and US$1,500 thresholds.

- Baccarat
- Craps
- Roulette
- Bix-6 wheel

If you win, and hopefully you will win real big, on any of the above games of chance, the Casino will NOT withhold any federal taxes. You might decide the best gambling strategy for you; taking into consideration the tax withholding (or lack of it in these circumstances) is to limit your play to blackjack, baccarat, craps, roulette or big 6-wheel. If you are looking for that big jackpot (e.g., the multi-million dollar jackpot from slot machines), you will need to deal with the 30% withholding tax explained in this book.[5]

D. Casinos and Race Tracks - Withholding at Source – Withholding by the Casino

At this point, you are probably asking yourself the question of what can I do to make sure the Casino does NOT withhold taxes on my jackpots or other games of chance winnings that are subject to withholding tax? The Casino surely views me as a good customer and will want me to continue to patronize their Casino and hence can be convinced not to withhold the 30% on the amounts of US$1,200 or more? If I ask them, plead with them, they will not withhold on my winnings?

In all cases, it is crucial that you request and maintain in your records all copies of Internal Revenue Service Forms

E. Why Casinos and Race Tracks Will Always Withhold

Unfortunately, for you as a non-U.S. citizen gambler, the methodology used by the IRS regarding withholding taxes, assures the Casino will always withhold. Indeed, Casinos and Race Tracks will withhold, even if they are not truly required to under the law, since the law specifically protects them from any legal claims or

[5] Many gamblers of these table games, particularly high roller high-stakes gamblers, simply will not play the slot machines or other games of chance, including placing bets at the Race Track, that give rise to the 30% withholding tax.

lawsuits a customer might wish to bring for any withholding taxes they collect and pay over directly to the U.S. Treasury.

If they do not withhold the 30% tax, the IRS can assert numerous penalties against Casinos and Race Tracks, including a so-called 100% penalty, equal to the amount of 30% of the winnings of their customer. There are other penalties they can be subject to, in addition to the 100% penalty, including failure to file penalties and failure to pay penalties among others. Accordingly, why would any Casino or Race Track ever NOT withhold, if they are protected under the law for withholding even if it was not required? They will always withhold.

Casinos and Race Tracks are protected by the U.S. tax law if they withhold taxes, even if they are not required under the law. On the other hand, they can be subject to penalties of more than 100% of the amount of 30% of the jackpots or other gambling winnings of its non-U.S. citizen clients for not withholding. Hence, Casinos will ALWAYS withhold 30% on any amounts of US$1,200 or greater.

CHAPTER 4
IRS APPROACH - THE *NON-SEQUITUR*

The author has already explained the basic principle how a non-resident gambler is subject to a 30% withholding tax on their "... periodical gains, profits, and income ..." sounds pretty simple. If a gambler has no "gains, profits and income" from their gambling, it would seem they should therefore not be subject to the 30% withholding tax. Unfortunately, the way this simple rule in the law has been administered by the IRS, is anything but simple, and imposes this 30% tax, even when the gambler has losses and has no "gains, profits and income."

According to the author, there is no comprehensive source of law for the propositions articulated by the Internal Revenue Service of how "gains, profits, and income" from gambling are to be determined. Instead, the Internal Revenue Service has merely published the following position in their internal writings:

> ***"Gambling winnings are subject to 30% withholding. Lottery winnings are not exempt. Winnings subject to withholding tax are not reduced by gambling losses. Gambling winnings are non-effectively connected unless documentation is submitted to prove an NRA is a professional gambler."***

Nowhere in that statement does it explain what is meant by "winnings" (incidentally, the term "winnings" does not appear in the statute) and what is meant by "gambling losses."[6] The imprecise

[6] The relevant portion of the statute is found in section 871(a)(1)(A), as it reads below:

> **§871. Tax on non-resident alien individuals**
>
> **(a) Income not connected with United States business—30 percent tax**
>
> **(1) Income other than capital gains**
>
> Except as provided in subsection (h), there is hereby imposed for each taxable year a tax of 30 percent of the amount received from sources within the United States by a non-resident alien individual as—
>
> > (A) interest (other than original issue discount as defined in section 1273), dividends, rents, salaries, wages, premiums, annuities, compensations, remunerations, emoluments, and other fixed or determinable annual or periodical ***gains, profits, and income***, ...
>
> [Emphasis added]

position of the Internal Revenue Service has simply been that each "per play" or purse and jackpot or winning of at least $1200, is subject to the 30% withholding tax. They then go on to describe the statutory law that provides that when someone is engaged in a "trade or business."[7] The IRS explains they are taxed in the same way as a United States resident, which means they are eligible for tax deductions and can reduce their income by ordinary trade or business expenses.[8]

The relevant portion of the withholding statute is section 1441(a), and reads as follows:

> **§1441. Withholding of tax on nonresident aliens**
>
> (a) General rule. Except as otherwise provided in subsection (c), all persons, in whatever capacity acting (including lessees or mortgagors of real or personal property, fiduciaries, employers, and all officers and employees of the United States) having the control, receipt, custody, disposal, or payment of any of the items of income specified in subsection (b) (to the extent that any of such items constitutes gross income from sources within the United States), of any nonresident alien individual or of any foreign partnership shall (except as otherwise provided in regulations prescribed by the Secretary under section 874) deduct and withhold from such items a tax equal to 30 percent thereof, except that in the case of any item of income specified in the second sentence of subsection (b), the tax shall be equal to 14 percent of such item.
>
> (b) Income items. The items of income referred to in subsection (a) are interest (other than original issue discount as defined in section 1273), dividends, rent, salaries, wages, premiums, annuities, compensations, remunerations, emoluments, or other fixed or determinable annual or periodical ***gains, profits, and income***, . . .
>
> [Emphasis added]

[7] The IRS uses the term "professional" or "professional gambler," which does not appear in the statute or law.

[8] The specific section regarding trade or business activities is section **871(b), Which reads in its entirety as follows:**

> **§871. Tax on non-resident alien individuals**
>
> **(b) Income connected with United States business—graduated rate of tax**
>
> **(1) Imposition of tax**
>
> A non-resident alien individual engaged in trade or business within the United States during the taxable year shall be taxable as provided in section 1 or 55 on his taxable income which is effectively connected with the conduct of a trade or business within the United States.
>
> **(2) Determination of taxable income**
>
> In determining taxable income for purposes of paragraph (1), gross income includes only gross income which is effectively connected with the conduct of a trade or business within the United States.

A. IRS – Ignore Basic Economics of Gambling Winnings and Investments of Non-U.S. Citizen Gamblers

The IRS' administration of this rule on a "per play" or "per spin" basis has turned the basic withholding tax rule on its head. The basic common sense approach used by the IRS with U.S. resident gamblers was "thrown out the window" when it comes to non-U.S. citizen, non-resident gamblers. U.S. players, at least of slot machines, are expressly authorized by the IRS to calculate their winnings and losses on a "per session" basis.[9]

The basic common sense approach used by the IRS with U.S. resident gamblers was "thrown out the window" when it comes to non-U.S. citizen, non-resident gamblers.

i. "Per Play" or "Per Spin" Versus "Per Session" Approach – the "INFINITE" Tax

The difference between a "per play" or "per spin" versus "per session" approach can be explained more clearly with a numerical analysis. Let's return to the example above of a single wager of US$500 that produces a payout of US$1,200; the economics of the two approaches can be simply demonstrated by adding another wager to the first wager. Assume the same gambler makes a second wager, shortly after placing the first wager and receiving a US$1,200 payout on that first spin. Of course, this gambler is thinking she is feeling lucky and could see even more

The IRS uses the term "professional" or "professional gambler," which does not appear in the statute or law.

[9] See, IRS Technical Advice Memorandum AM2008-11, Office of Chief Counsel, Internal Revenue Service 4 (2008). There, the IRS explained, using basic common sense, that "We think that the fluctuating wins and losses left in play are not accessions to wealth until the taxpayer redeems her tokens and can definitively calculate" her gains. The IRS went on to say in the case of U.S. resident slot machine players, that a "taxpayer who plays the slot machines recognizes a wagering gain or loss at the time she redeems her tokens."

payouts. In the second wager, therefore, she places a bet of US$1,000.

Unfortunately, on the second wager, our gambler was not so lucky and had a zero pay out of such second spin. The following mathematical calculation of the second wager transaction (e.g., "second pull of the slot machine" or "second wager at the Race Track") is set forth below:

Wager No. 2	Combined	
Jackpot or Race Winning Amounts		$0
AMOUNT WAGERED		$(1,000)
"Loss" from Wagering Transactions		**$(1,000)**
U.S. Federal Withholding Tax Rate (30%)	30%	
U.S. Federal Withholding Tax (Paid by Casino or Race Track to IRS)		$0
Nothing to Gambler	$0	N/A ($0)
"Loss" from Wager Transactions after Taxes Paid	$0 Win Amount, Less $1,000 Amount Wagered	$(1,000)
Effective Tax Rate on Profit from Wager Transactions		NA

At this point, you are probably starting to see where this calculation is heading; and it is not looking good for the non-U.S. citizen gambler.

In this example, the first wager at least returned a payoff to the gambler, to more than offset the 30% withholding tax paid directly by the Casino or the Race Track to the IRS. Of course, the second wager put the non-resident gambler in a hole; in the negative; in the red, or whatever term you like to use to say the results of the gambling losses are now causing severe losses due to the 30% tax withheld and paid over to the IRS on the first wager. The rest of this book is focused on how to get that 30% withholding tax ($360 in the example) back from the IRS.

ii. How the IRS Defines "Gains, Profits and Income" – the *Non-Sequitur*

The Court in *Sang Park*, identified the glaring *non-sequitur* from the method by which the IRS determines "losses and winnings in the first place" for non-resident gamblers. In short, the basic language of the law that imposes the 30% withholding tax on ". . . periodical gains, profits, and income . . ." has been interpreted by the IRS to mean "gains, profits and income" on each and every successful bet. They do not measure these gains and profits over the session of the gambling activity and they do not allow an adjustment for the amounts wagered or placed into the machine or at the Race Track.

The Court in *Sang Park*, identified the glaring non-sequitur from the method by which the IRS determines "losses and winnings in the first place" for non-resident gamblers. In short, the basic language of the law that imposes the 30% withholding tax on ". . . periodical gains, profits, and income . . ." has been interpreted by the IRS to mean "gains, profits and income" on each and every successful bet. They do not measure these gains and profits over the session of the gambling activity and they do not allow an adjustment for the amounts wagered or placed into the machine.

As we continue on with our example of the gambler who placed just two wagers in a single session (e.g., US$500 on bet number 1, and $1,000 on bet number 2), the IRS' "per spin" or "per bet" or "per play" approach gets shown under the harsh light of basic economics of what the IRS apparently considers "gains, profits and income." By combining both of only two bets in this example, the following numerical calculation demonstrates the *non-sequitur*:

Wager No. 1 & No. 2	**Combined**	
Jackpot or Race Winning Amounts		$1,200
AMOUNTS WAGERED		**$(1,500)**
"Loss" from Wagering Transactions		**$(300)**
U.S. Federal Withholding Tax Rate (30%)	30%	
U.S. Federal Withholding Tax (Paid by Casino or Race Track to IRS)		$360
Balance to Gambler	**$1,200 Win Amount, Less $360 Taxes, Less Wagered Amounts**	N/A ($0)
"Loss" from Wagering Transactions after Taxes Paid	$1,200 Win Amount, Less $1,500 Amount Wagered, Less $360 Taxes	$(660)
Effective Tax Rate on "Loss" from Wager Transactions	$300 "Loss" Relative to $360 of Taxes Withheld	* Infinite

Notice the negatives throughout these calculations. Negative numbers are not good for the gambler or any activity where money is put at risk. Amazingly, the effective tax rate imposed on the gambler in these two wagers is "infinite." The tax rate is "infinite" since paying tax on zero winnings should yield zero taxes. Here, the IRS claims a tax owed on the gambler's gains, profits and income! Yes, she has none. In other words, the gambler, paid the U.S. federal government taxes (indirectly via the 30% withholding imposed on the first wager that was withheld and paid directly by the Casino or Race Track) when she had no actual "gains, profits and income". The author is of the view, that under no reasonable standard, would someone walk away from the above determination and conclude this gambler had any "gains, profits and income." The IRS' application of the law concludes otherwise. Hence, the *non-sequitur.*

Take our above example one step further; applying the IRS method, we can see how extreme the tax results are for the gambler. Let's assume the non-resident gambler thinks that if she places one more bet (a third wager), she can get back her losses and earn some profit, or at least go home "even." Hence, she wages $1,000 again, on the third wager, which produces a jackpot of US$1,350. The following table summarizes the results, including a 30% withholding tax of US$405 on the US$1,350 jackpot.

Wager No. 3		
Jackpot or Race Winning Amount		$1,350
AMOUNT WAGERED		$(1,000)
"Win" from Wager Transaction		**$350**
U.S. Federal Withholding Tax Rate (30%)	30%	-
U.S. Federal Withholding Tax (Paid by Casino or Race Track to IRS)		$405
Nothing to Gambler	**$0**	**N/A ($0)**
"Loss" from Wager Transaction after Taxes Paid	$ 1,350 "Win" Amount, Less $1,000 Amount Wagered, Less US$405 Taxes	$(55)
Effective Tax Rate on Profit from Wager Transaction	$350 "Profit" Relative to $405 of Taxes Withheld	116%

You will notice that the effect of the withholding tax is that all gain from the wagering transaction (more than 100% of it; 116% of it) is paid over to the IRS on this third wager only.

The consequence of all three wagers combined, shows the net effect of all three wagers as follows:

Wager No. 1 & No. 2 & No. 3	Combined	
Jackpot or Race Winning Amounts		$2,550
AMOUNTS WAGERED		$ (2,500)
"Gain" from Wagering Transactions		**$50**
U.S. Federal Withholding Tax Rate (30%)	30%	-
U.S. Federal Withholding Tax (Paid by Casino or Race Track to IRS)	30% of $2,550	$765
Balance to Gambler	**$2,550 Win Amounts, Less $765 Taxes, Less Wagered Amounts of $2,500**	N/A ($0)
"Loss" from Wagering Transactions after Taxes Paid	$2,550 Win Amount, Less $2,500 Amount Wagered, Less $765 Taxes	$(715)
Effective Tax Rate on "Gain" from Wager Transactions	$50 "Gain" Relative to $765 of Taxes Withheld	1530%

The IRS *non-sequitur* approach, takes a modest gain from all three wagers in that session of US$50, and imposes total withholding tax of US$715. This has the effect of a U.S. effective income tax rate of 1,530%. This is NOT a typo!

Of course, the Court in *Sang Park* would reflect the three wagers in a single session, and conclude that "gains, profits and income" of US$50 was earned by the non-resident gambler. A 30% withholding tax on the US$50 of "gains, profits and income" produces a $15 total tax, as opposed to the IRS approach of US715. You will notice the stark difference between the two amounts.

Fortunately, for non-resident gamblers around the world, the U.S. Court of Appeals for the District of Columbia Circuit in the *Sang Park* decision soundly rejected the IRS calculation of gains, profits and income in this context. This leaves the non-resident gambler with only one choice to recover taxes they should have never owed in the first place. It must bring a refund action against the Internal Revenue Service under the law.

Fortunately, for non-resident gamblers around the world, the U.S. Court of Appeals for the District of Columbia Circuit in the *Sang Park* decision soundly rejected the IRS calculation of gains, profits and income for recreational non-resident gamblers.

CHAPTER 5
WHY DOES THIS CONFUSION AND "ECONOMIC MADNESS" EXIST IN HOW THE IRS ADMINISTERS AND CALCULATES THE GAINS, PROFITS AND INCOME OF A NON-RESIDENT GAMBLER?

If you think this whole system does not make any sense, you're not alone. But why does the Internal Revenue Service insist on continuing to impose the withholding tax in the manner it does against Casinos and Race Tracks?

A. Driven by Government Reports and Critiques?

The answer to this question is very complex. If there was a simple logical answer, there would probably be no reason to read or write this book. Unfortunately, the Internal Revenue Service has administered the withholding tax on non-resident gamblers under the non sequitur method for reasons that are hard to explain or understand. This is an attempt to explain probably why this system continues unabated at the Internal Revenue Service. First, the government itself probably does not understand that the $1,200 threshold does not exist in the law, the statute or the regulations. This $1,200 on non-resident jackpots and Race Track winnings is probably presumed (erroneously) to be the law even at the Internal Revenue Service.

The government itself probably does not understand that the $1,200 threshold does not exist in the law, the statute or the regulations.

Second, there are a number of procedural safeguards the Internal Revenue Service has and that it imposes prior to issuing a tax refund for a non-resident gambler. These requirements are extensive and commonly create a major roadblock for the non-resident to be able to recover the withholding taxes that should have never been withheld in the first place. Without going into great detail of each procedural requirement, it is worth saying that these requirements commonly prevent a non-resident gambler from ever being able to legally recover taxes withheld at source by the Casino or Race Track without bringing a lawsuit against the U.S. Treasury. See IRM 3.38.147.7.5 (01-01-2013) Gambling Income.

You will notice that there is no reference to statutes, regulations or other law in the non-resident gambling section in the IRM. The relevant provisions of the IRM which is used by the personnel of the Internal Revenue Service as the "tax Bible" states as follows:

> ***"Gambling winnings are subject to 30% withholding. Lottery winnings are not exempt. Winnings subject to withholding tax are not reduced by gambling losses. Gambling winnings are non-effectively connected unless documentation is submitted to prove an NRA [non-resident alien] is a professional gambler."***

As previously explained, the application of this rule will typically yield an ***infinite tax rate***, since gambling can easily produce no profits or gains; yet when a tax is imposed on those losses, the result produces a positive. The effective tax rate is an ***infinite*** number. To say it another way, a positive number multiplied by a negative number, can never produce a positive result. However, that is exactly what the IRS determination of tax does when a gambler has a loss. It takes a positive number, the tax withheld, multiplied by a negative number, the loss incurred by the gambler, and that multiple is left with a positive; i.e., the tax paid over to the IRS by the Casino. This ***infinite tax rate*** is, of course, the *non-sequitur.*

The application of this rule will typically yield an "infinite" tax rate – whenever the gambler has no economic winnings.

B. Treasury Inspector General's Report – Re: Non-Resident Gamblers

To make matters worse, there was a Treasury Inspector General's report for tax administration issued in 2010 critiquing the procedures and methods used by the Internal Revenue Service regarding tax refunds for non-resident gamblers. The Treasury Inspector General is a sort of "watchdog" over the activities of the Internal Revenue Service. See full report - *Improvements Are Needed to Verify Refunds to*

Non-Resident Aliens Before the Refunds Are Sent Out of the United States The Inspector General.[10]

Unfortunately, that report was poorly written in the author's view, and most importantly, did not attempt to look into or try to explain the withholding tax law as it applies to non-resident gamblers. Instead, the report merely assumes that the thresholds of withholding at $1200 are allowed and provided for under the law. It assumes the IRS properly determines "gains, profits and income" for the correct withholding of taxes on non-resident gamblers. The report further frets that the Internal Revenue Service may be allowing non-resident gamblers to recover money to which they are not owed. Accordingly, the result of the Internal Revenue Service is to deny, deny and further deny federal tax withholding refunds for non-resident gamblers. This puts you as the non-resident gambler living somewhere around the world at a terrible disadvantage when you need to go up against Goliath, the Taxman.

That report did not attempt to look into or try to explain the withholding tax law as it applies to non-resident gamblers.

C. More Than Just the Taxman

One of the other big roadblocks that affect the administration of withholding tax for non-resident gamblers has nothing to do with the tax law. Rather, the "Taxman," Internal Revenue Service, is joined by his United States Treasury Department brethren in trying to identify and locate illegal money laundering activities. While you are trying to win big at games of chance in US Race Tracks and Casinos, the various departments in the Treasury Department including the financial

Various departments in the Treasury Department including the financial crimes enforcement network ("FinCEN") are looking for money laundering of funds by all persons, including non-residents gamblers.

[10] http://www.treasury.gov/tigta/auditreports/2010reports/201040121fr.pdf.

crimes enforcement network ("FinCEN") are looking for money laundering of funds by all persons, including non-residents gamblers. As you can imagine, the law of money laundering will take precedence over the administration of tax and tax refunds.

The federal anti-money laundering regulations include a Casino as an organization that is required to issue certain currency transaction reports. These regulations require that each Casino file a report of each transaction in currency, involving either "cash in" or "cash out," of more than US$10,000.[11]

You can see that the U.S. Casino and Race Track has to worry about more than just the Taxman and the 30% withholding tax, since during the same time it is issuing information reports regarding each of the above currency transactions for anti-money laundering purposes.

---

[11] These rules define CASH-IN transactions to include but not limited to:

A.Purchases of Casino chips, tokens and other gaming instruments

B.Deposit(s) (front money or safekeeping)

C.Payments in any form of credit including markers and counter checks

D.Bets of currency

E.Currency received by the Casino for transmittal of funds through wire transfer for a customer

F.Purchases of Casino checks

G.Exchanges of currency for currency including foreign currency

H.Bills inserted into electronic gaming devices

CASH-OUT transactions include but are not limited to:

A.Redemption of Casino chips, tokens, tickets, and other gaming instruments

B.Withdrawal(s) of deposit (front money)

C.Safekeeping withdrawals

D.Advances on any form of credit, including markers and counter checks

E.Payments on bets

F.Payments by a Casino to a customer based on receipt of funds through wire transfer

G.Cashing of checks or other negotiable instruments

H.Currency exchanges, including foreign currency

I.Travel and complimentary expenses and gaming incentives

J.Payment for tournament, contests, and other promotions

CHAPTER 6
RECORDKEEPING – GREAT IMPORTANCE

If there is only one single item that you should take away from this book, it is the importance of good record keeping in your gambling endeavors. Many a case against the IRS has been won or lost based upon good or bad recordkeeping, respectively. You have the burden of proof under the law to demonstrate and account for your gambling activities. You will need to demonstrate three basic items:

You have the burden of proof under the law, to demonstrate and account for your gambling activities.

(i) The amount of funds used to gamble;
(ii) The amount of jackpots or race winnings won; and
(iii) The amount of U.S. federal withholding tax (the 30% tax) withheld by the Casino or the Race Track.

At first blush, this might appear to be fairly simple and straightforward. However, usually gamblers are notoriously bad about keeping good records and accountings for their gambling activities. All of the wagered amounts must be kept for the gambling activities. There are a couple methods by which one can keep track their amounts wagered. The first and most accurate and comprehensive (and by all standards the most impractical approach) is to track every single wager. For the Race Track gambler, such approach is not so impractical and can be monitored with each wager placed. However, those who each play Keno, slot machines or other similar gambling devices, cannot practically keep track of wager, especially when each wager placed maybe takes 20 to 40 seconds.

Similarly, on the winning side of the equation, all of the Winnings and Jackpot amounts must be tracked for the gambling activities. There are a couple methods by which one can keep track of the Winnings and Jackpot amounts. The first and most accurate and comprehensive (and by all standards the most impractical approach) is to track every single winning and jackpot amount. For the Race Track gambler, such approach is not so impractical and can be monitored with each winning amount. However, those who play Keno, slot machines or other similar gambling devices, cannot practically keep track of Jackpot amounts, especially when they maybe are won every 2 to 3 minutes of play.

The alternative approach is to track with great detail the gross amounts wagered during a playing session and the gross amounts of winnings and jackpot amounts. The difference between those two amounts will represent the "gains, profits, and income" or (ii) loss during a particular session. A daily log or journal should ideally be kept.

This latter approach requires a good control system to ensure that funds spent between the beginning and end of the gambling session are accounted for separately. For instance, let's assume you start with $1,500 at the beginning of the gambling session. You gamble for three hours and at the end of the session you have $900. If someone does not think too much about the accounting for these amounts, the gambler might believe they have a loss of $600 ($1,500 which they started with –less - $900 dollars, the amount they ended with). If the gambler did nothing in between the three hour time periods, the loss might be accurate, depending upon the 30% withheld tax, if any. However, if the gambler ate lunch for $22, made a gift of $300 to her husband who was also at the Casino, and provided $75 to her children, all while gambling during that three hour period, her loss would be $397 less (representing the amounts she spent in that three hour session); in other words only $207 would be her loss. She might even have a gain if more than $207 of taxes were withheld.

All gamblers should track:

- **How much money you gambled.**
- **How much money you won gambling.**
- **How much you spent trying to win at gambling (if you are in the "trade or business" of gambling)**

Modifying slightly the facts in this example, let's assume at the end of the gambling session of three hours she has $1,400 left in her pocket. At first blush, she might think she had a loss of $100. ($1,500 which they started with – less than $1,400 left in their pocket at the end of the gambling session.) However, we know that she actually has a gain of at least $297 since her apparent loss of $100 must be increased by $397 the amount she spent to eat lunch for $22, the gift of $300 to her husband who was also in the Casino, and the $75 she provided to her children. If taxes were withheld, her profit would be increased by the amount of these withheld taxes.

In addition, expenses associated with your gambling activities should be tracked.

The importance of how much you spent trying to win at gambling, these trade or business expenses, help determine your final taxable income or whether you might have a loss. You have to keep detailed records of all of these amounts and items if you want to ultimately prevail against the Internal Revenue Service.

A. Burden of Proof of the Gambler – Taxpayer

Many people are surprised to learn that the burden of proof lies with the taxpayer. Too many movies regarding criminal burdens of proof, probably lead many gamblers and people in the public at large, to believe that the government has to prove the tax liability of the individual in a civil tax case. This is not the case, and the gambler has the burden of proof. The law expressly provides that the determination made by the Internal Revenue Service of the amount of tax owing is presumed to be correct. This presumption in favor of the Internal Revenue Service is rebuttable by the taxpayer/gambler, but the taxpayer must carry this burden.

The law expressly provides that the determination made by the Internal Revenue Service of the amount of tax owing is presumed to be correct. This presumption in favor of the Internal Revenue Service is rebuttable by the taxpayer/gambler, but the taxpayer must carry this burden.

That is why your books and records and accurate information about how much you gambled, how much you won and how much you spent gambling (if you are in the trade or business of gambling) is so important. Without decent records, the Internal Revenue Service is bound to prevail and you may (probably will) lose your suit for a refund to recover the taxes that are legally owed to you.

B. "Coin-In" and "Coin-Out"

There are some important terms that are used in wagering that are of great importance for the recordkeeping for each gambler. In games such as slot machines and keno, the term "coin-in" simply means the total amount of actual wagers; or amounts played. The term "coin-out" reflects the amount of winnings from the gambling activity. The terminology is a throwback to the days when slot machines actually took and paid out real coins.

In the past, these older coin machines (which have largely been phased out of U.S. Casinos in the past several years) would physically pay out jackpots and winnings in coins. Now, virtually all machines never pay out jackpots in actual coins, but rather pay tickets. The tickets are barcoded slips of paper that can be redeemed for cash or inserted into other machines for more play. The change in technology has not eliminated the terminology of "coin-in" and "coin-out".

The concept sounds simple enough. However, it is not always easy to track the "coin-in" and "coin-out" amounts of slot machines; particularly if the gambler is placing dozens, hundreds or even thousands of bets in a day.

C. Players Card – Its Importance

The Players card is a small credit card size plastic device that is inserted into the slot machines. It electronically tracks all play and gambling activity that is made at that machine(s) where it was used, which includes all "coin in" and all "coin

The Casino will be able to track the times of play, the machines gambled, and all other economic activity at the slot machine with the players' card.

out." The Casino will be able to track the times of play, the machines gambled, and all other economic activity at the slot machine with the players' card. Casinos generally provide points or special bonus promotions for players who utilize their players' card. There is a little known trick, that sometimes the machine may not read the players card and it is therefore important that when inserted, the machine is functioning properly and reading the gambling activity and reflect it appropriately on the players card. The U.S. Tax Court has determined that there is an important legal significance of records and data produced by a player's card. At least some Courts in the United States have found that it is the best way to account for all gambling activities, including "coin in" and all "coin out."

D. Contemporaneous ("at the Time") Records

In addition to players' card activity, it is best to keep contemporaneous ("at the time") records of each gambling session. Those record should reflect how much is gambled during the session, how much in winnings, and how much cash you had prior to the gambling session and after the gambling session ended. A daily journal recording these activities is the best method to track your gambling activities.

E. Loans – "Markers"

You will also need to account for how much you borrowed and how much was drawn against credit cards, checks, ATMs, or loans made by the Casino to you for gambling play. You want to make sure you track the use of those funds and can demonstrate that they were used for gambling, or if not, for what other purposes. Of course, the Casino specifically calls their loans to their clients - "markers".

It is best to keep contemporaneous ("at the time") records of each gambling session.

CHAPTER 7
CASUAL GAMBLERS VERSUS THOSE IN A TRADE OR BUSINESS OF GAMBLING

There is a big difference in the tax law, whether a non-resident gambler is a mere (i) casual or recreational gambler (which represents the vast majority of gamblers), or (ii) is engaged in a so-called "trade or business" of gambling. Sometimes the term "recreational" gambler is used for "casual" gambler and the term "professional" is used for a gambler engaged in a "trade or business."

A. Important Distinction - U.S. Supreme Court – *Groetzinger* Standard

Those who are engaged in a trade or business (the so-called "professional" gambler) must be able to satisfy and eventually prove in the event of an IRS audit, that they are involved in the gambling activity with (i) continuity and regularity; and (ii) the primary purpose of engaging in gambling for income or profit. If these rules sound technical and legal, it's because they are. The United States Supreme Court ruled, in the most important case in this area - *Comm'r v. Groetzinger*[12], the gambler, needed to be (i) continuously and regularly engaged in gambling and (ii) for the primary purpose of making a profit. If both criteria are satisfied, the gambler would be in the trade or business and not a mere casual gambler. In that case, *Groetzinger*, the gambler won.

The tax difference between a "casual" versus "trade or business" gamblers is very significant. A casual gambler cannot deduct various expenses associated with gambling; e.g., traveling to and from the Casinos, qualifying meals and entertainment, telephone/internet, handicapping data, books and research materials that are purchased or expended by the gambler., etc. A casual non-resident gambler

The tax difference between a "casual" versus "trade or business" gamblers is very significant.

[12] 480 U.S. 23 (1987).

must also generally calculate their "gains, profits and income" utilizing a "per session" approach as opposed to accounting for all gambling activity during the course of the entire year. The economic differences between these two approaches are discussed and explained in more detail below (*See*, ***Determining Taxable Income (or Loss) for a Gambler in a Trade or Business & Determining Taxable Income for a Casual or Recreational Gambler***). Whether you are a gambler dedicated to a trade or business or a casual gambler, the Casinos and Race Tracks in the United States will nevertheless withhold the 30% withholding tax on the gross jackpot or race earnings of US$1,200 or more. The interplay of this withholding tax and the method by which taxable income is determined for both types of non-resident gamblers are discussed in more detail below.

B. Determining Taxable Income for a Gambler in a Trade or Business

Most importantly, the calculation of "income" is quite different for the casual gambler where the law defines "gains, profits and income". The gambler engaged in a trade or business, in contrast, falls into a different set of rules. If all of the expenses exceed the gross receipts from the gambling activity, there will be no profit or taxable income upon which to pay any U.S. income tax.

Most significantly, a gambler in the trade or business of gambling can deduct all ordinary and necessary business expenses.

The law characterizes this "trade or business" activity as income of a non-resident that is "effectively connected with the conduct of a trade or business in the United States". This means, the taxable income must be calculated generally in the same manner and at the same tax rates as that of a U.S. gambler engaged in a trade or business.[13]

This requires the trade or business gambler to file a United States income tax return (IRS Form 1040NR). The taxpayer is to attach an

[13] *See*, I.R.C. § 871(b) and § 1.

IRS Form, ***Schedule C, Profit or Loss From Business (Sole Proprietorship)***[14] reporting all losses and expenses, which offset and reduce the gambling income. The initial part of page one of this form is set out below for the reader to have an idea of some of the information to be reported on the U.S. income tax return:

[14] See, http://www.irs.gov/pub/irs-pdf/f1040sc.pdf for IRS Form Schedule C.

SCHEDULE C (Form 1040)

Department of the Treasury
Internal Revenue Service (99)

Profit or Loss From Business

(Sole Proprietorship)

▶ **For information on Schedule C and its instructions, go to *www.irs.gov/schedulec*.**

▶ **Attach to Form 1040, 1040NR, or 1041; partnerships generally must file Form 1065.**

OMB No. 1545-0074

2012

Attachment Sequence No. **09**

Name of proprietor | **Social security number (SSN)**

A Principal business or profession, including product or service (see instructions) | **B Enter code from instructions** ▶

C Business name. If no separate business name, leave blank. | **D Employer ID number (EIN)**, (see instr.)

E Business address (including suite or room no.) ▶

City, town or post office, state, and ZIP code

F Accounting method: **(1)** ☐ Cash **(2)** ☐ Accrual **(3)** ☐ Other (specify) ▶

G Did you "materially participate" in the operation of this business during 2012? If "No," see instructions for limit on losses . ☐ **Yes** ☐ **No**

H If you started or acquired this business during 2012, check here . . . . ▶ ☐

I Did you make any payments in 2012 that would require you to file Form(s) 1099? (see instructions) . . . . ☐ **Yes** ☐ **No**

J If "Yes," did you or will you file required Forms 1099? . . . . ☐ **Yes** ☐ **No**

Part I Income

1	Gross receipts or sales. See instructions for line 1 and check the box if this income was reported to you on Form W-2 and the "Statutory employee" box on that form was checked . . . . ▶ ☐	1	
2	Returns and allowances (see instructions)	2	
3	Subtract line 2 from line 1	3	

The Internal Revenue Service forms can be very confusing and complicated. This is not an attempt to try to explain all of the nuances and complexities of these forms. However, it is important to know the basic procedures and requirements. The Internal Revenue Service schedule C is used for all gamblers who are engaged in a trade or business of gambling; both resident gamblers and non-resident gamblers like you.

The next form is Internal Revenue Service Form W2G. This form is sometimes confused and issued for non-resident gamblers incorrectly by the Casinos and Race Tracks. This is wrong and an incorrect procedure. This form is only to be used for US resident gamblers.

You as a non-resident gambler should never receive this form W2G. The correct form for you to receive as a non-resident is Internal Revenue Service Form 1042-S.

This IRS form is <u>not to be used</u> with or for non-resident gamblers. This form is applicable to United States taxpayers including those who reside and live in the United States.

3232 ☐ VOID ☐ CORRECTED

PAYER'S name, street address, city or town, province or state, country, ZIP or foreign postal code	1 Gross winnings $	2 Date won	OMB No. 1545-0238 2013 **Form W-2G** **Certain Gambling Winnings**
	3 Type of wager	4 Federal income tax withheld $	
	5 Transaction	6 Race	
	7 Winnings from identical wagers $	8 Cashier	
Federal identification number / Telephone number	9 Winner's taxpayer identification no.	10 Window	
WINNER'S name	11 First I.D.	12 Second I.D.	For Privacy Act and Paperwork Reduction Act Notice, see the **2013 General Instructions for Certain Information Returns.**
Street address (including apt. no.)	13 State/Payer's state identification no.	14 State winnings $	
City or town, province or state, country, and ZIP or foreign postal code	15 State income tax withheld $	16 Local winnings $	**File with Form 1096**
	17 Local income tax withheld $	18 Name of locality	**Copy A For Internal Revenue Service Center**

Under penalties of perjury, I declare that, to the best of my knowledge and belief, the name, address, and taxpayer identification number that I have furnished correctly identify me as the recipient of this payment and any payments from identical wagers, and that no other person is entitled to any part of these payments.

Signature ▶ **Date ▶**

Form **W-2G** Cat. No. 10138V www.irs.gov/w2g Department of the Treasury - Internal Revenue Service

Do Not Cut or Separate Forms on This Page – Do Not Cut or Separate Forms on This Page

A basic summary of how a gambler in a trade or business will calculate their taxable income is set forth below. The accounting and calculations are made for a calendar year, irrespective of your tax year in your home country, and are based upon total gross winnings (e.g., jackpots), total bets placed, other income (e.g., "comps" – discussed below later), and are then reduced by trade or business expenses such as airfare, hotel, and expenses incurred developing gaming strategies and working with professional advisors.

The following is a basic example and calculation of how a trade or business gambler will report their final taxable income from gambling activities:

Gambler with Trade or Business Schedule of Taxable Income			
Total Gross Winnings	Gross Receipts	$190,405	
Total Best placed	- "Wagers"	($169,737)	
Other Income – "Comps" (Indirect)		$1,297	
	Gross Profit		$21,966
Trade or Business Expenses			
Airfare		$2,323	
Hotel		3,653	
Professional – Accountant/Lawyers		718	
Meals & entertainment		1,651	
Telephone & Internet		670	
Admission/Entry fees		1,251	
Subscriptions		1,056	
Conferences on Gaming Strategies		98	
Literature on Gaming Strategies		$52	
	Trade or Business Expenses		($11,472)
Taxable Income			**$10,494**

In the above example, the taxpayer has taxable income from her gambling activities of US$10,494. As previously said, the law provides that a non-resident, who is engaged in a trade or business in the United States, is generally taxed in the same manner and at the same rates as a U.S. resident taxpayer. Hence, a U.S. resident gambler would have taxable income calculated in the same manner as the non-resident gambler. Both would have US$10,494 of taxable income in the same above example. Incidentally, the tax rate on that modest amount of taxable income would be less than 10% for total taxes owed to the U.S. of less than $1,495.

> **The law provides that a non-resident, who is engaged in a trade or business in the United States, is generally taxed in the same manner and at the same rates as a U.S. resident taxpayer. Hence, a U.S. resident gambler would have taxable income calculated in the same manner as the non-resident gambler.**

As we know, gamblers cannot always have a profitable year. Accordingly, if the same gambler, engaged in a trade or business incurs greater expenses in the same taxable year, the following is an example of how the gambler would calculate his or her loss:

Gambler with Trade or Business Schedule of Taxable Income			
Total Gross Winnings	Gross Receipts	$120,463	
Total Best placed	- "Wagers"	($131,760)	
	Gross Profit (Loss)		($11,297)
Trade or Business Expenses (Indirect)			
Car and truck		$3,109	
Interest		91	
Office		256	
Travel		776	
Meals & entertainment		1,651	
Telephone & Internet		670	
Admission/Entry fees		1,251	
Subscriptions		1,056	
Handicapping data		1,960	
ATM Fees		$148	
Trade or Business Expenses (Still Deductible Under Section 162)			($10,968)
Loss from Gambling Trade or Business			(22,265)
Taxable Income			**$0**
Trade or Business Expenses (Deductible Under Section 162 not limited by 165(d))			($10,968)

In this example, the gambler incurs a loss of ($22,265), but has taxable income of US$0. Importantly, the tax law does not allow the taxpayer to take the gambling loss from the direct wages to offset against other taxable income he or she might have in the U.S.

There is an important wrinkle in the law that benefits the U.S. trade or business gambler that has other related gambling expenses. In this example, the wagers were ($131,760) which created a wagering loss from the direct gambling activities of ($11,297). In addition, there were trade or business expenses related to the gambling activity of ($10,965) (e.g., meals and entertainment, telephone, entry fees, handicapping data, etc.).

The U.S. Tax Court[15] has clarified the rule that a gambler engaged in a trade or business cannot deduct wagering losses against other income.[16] However, very importantly, the Court clarified that certain expenses "incidental to gambling" are not subject to this limitation and can therefore be deducted against other taxable income. The Internal Revenue Service has agreed that it will follow the opinion of that case and allow deductions of gambling related expenses, even if the losses incurred from such expenses exceed the losses caused directly related from gambling wagers. This case dealt with a resident gambler, but since the law says that non-resident gamblers engaged in a trade or business of gambling, should be treated the same as resident gamblers, the same rules should apply to you as a non-resident gambler.

If this sounds confusing; it is! The good news is that anyone who is a non-resident, who has a trade or business of gambling, can deduct and offset the expenses related to gambling (e.g., travel, meals and entertainment, subscriptions, telephone & intent, handicapping data expenses, etc.) against other income that is otherwise taxable in the U.S. For a non-resident gambler, this rule will not be of any use, if they do not have other U.S. sources of income subject to U.S. income taxation (e.g., U.S. real estate that they own). If the non-resident gambler has other U.S. activities (e.g., U.S. rental real estate

The good news is that anyone who is a non-resident, who has a trade or business of gambling, can deduct and offset the expenses related to gambling (e.g., travel, meals and entertainment, subscriptions, telephone & intent, handicapping data expenses, etc.) against other income that is otherwise taxable in the U.S.

---

[15] See, *Mayo v. Commissioner*, 136 T.C. 81 (2011), which cited to the 9th Circuit Appellate Decision in *Boyd v. United States*, 762 F.2d 1369 (9th Cir. 1985), and stated "The Court of Appeals distinguished between wagering losses and "expenses incidental to gambling", observing that the latter "would not be subject to the section 165(d) deduction limit." *Id.* at 1372.

[16] See, IRC Section 165(d), which imposes this limitation.

income or gains from the sale of U.S. real estate), then he or she can generally reduce that other non-gambling income from the U.S. real estate by the gambling related expenses.

C. In a Trade or Business Recordkeeping is Most Important

For gamblers, who are engaged in a trade or business, all receipts of expenses that may be related to the business of gambling should be maintained and kept as part of the gambler's accountings. These expenses would include items such as:

- Hotel stay/lodging at or near the Casino or Race Track where the gambler needed to travel to in order to gamble.
- Meals and entertainment related to the gambling activities; e.g., meals consumed at the Casino or Race Track while gambling.
- Books, journals and other research materials regarding gambling, gambling techniques and strategies.
- Fees paid to bookkeepers, legal accounting and tax advisors regarding laws, regulations and requirements surrounding gaming, accountings and tax requirements under the law.
- Travel expenses to the Casinos or Race Tracks.

In addition, gamblers in a trade or business should ideally maintain separate bank accounts used exclusively for gambling activities. This account can start with the initial capital to pay for trade or business expenses and to place wagers. In addition, all winnings and jackpots should ideally be deposited in the trade or business gambling account. Of course, since you are not a resident of the U.S., you will probably find it much easier to use your bank account in your country of residence. Nowadays, it will probably be nearly impossible for you to open a bank account in the U.S., due to the banking due diligence requirements and restrictions on opening accounts for foreign

In addition, gamblers in a trade or business should ideally maintain separate bank accounts used exclusively for gambling activities.

persons. The USA Patriot Act and due diligence imposed by the Bank Secrecy Act of the United States, makes it nearly impossible for non-resident aliens to open bank accounts in the United States.

For all of the above reasons, non-resident gamblers can typically more easily manage their cash flow from gambling wagers and winnings through "markers" (loans) taken from the Casino or Race Track. Having access to lines of credit directly from the Casino or Race Track, usually facilitates all trade or business activities and gambling and helps you better keep track of your own accounting records for tax purposes.

D. Determining Taxable Income for a Casual or Recreational Gambler

For a U.S. resident taxpayer's gambling activity that does not constitute a trade or business, his or her gambling losses are still deductible as an itemized deduction in arriving at their taxable income. These U.S. resident taxpayer's gambling activities with losses are reported on Schedule A.[17] A deduction for losses from gambling transactions is allowed to the extent of gains from such transactions, for U.S. resident taxpayer's recreational gambling activity.[18]

In contrast, non-resident recreational gamblers must calculate their income in a manner very differently than any other category of gamblers, which includes those in a U.S. trade or business – both resident and non-resident; and those U.S. resident recreational gamblers. They do not get to deduct "trade" or "business" expenses that a professional gambler may deduct. The following table provides an overview of the different systems:

---

[17] I.R.C. § 63(a). See, IRS Form Schedule A at www.irs.gov.

[18] I.R.C. § 165(d); Treas. Reg. § 1.165-10.

	U.S. TRADE OR BUSINESS – "PROFESSIONAL" GAMBLERS	Casual – Recreational Gamblers
Resident	Same as Non-Residents	Cumulative Losses Offset Gains-Income
Non-Resident	Same as Residents	No Offset for Cumulative Losses vis-à-vis Gains-Income

The non-resident casual gambler falls within the least desirable income tax regimes for gamblers in the United States. Also, the IRS's view of the law clashes head on with the law as explained by the Court in *Sang Park*. The IRS' view is that whatever the Casino or Race Track withholds on each winning spin or best (i.e., on all winning amounts of at least US$1,200) that is the final tax owing. The Court in *Sang Park*, however, overturned the IRS' determination of taxation on this "per spin" approach. The law is to utilize the "per session" approach to determine "income, gains or profit", which means that all wagers (per spin/per play) that generate a loss in such session is to be off-set against the cumulative total of all jackpots or winnings during that session.

The IRS' view is that whatever the Casino or Race Track withholds on each winning spin or best (i.e., on all winning amounts of at least US$1,200) that is the final tax owing.

The following illustration of 25 wagers by a recreational gambler in a particular session demonstrates the difference in results of the IRS approach and the law as described in *Sang Park*. This illustration shows various jackpots ranging from US$200 to US$8,000, where the

30% withholding tax is imposed upon only those jackpots or winning amounts of at least US$1,200.

Wager No.	Wagered Amounts	Cumulative Wagered Amounts	Jackpot Amount	Cumulative Jackpot Amounts	Withholding Tax Amounts	Cumulative Withholding Tax Amounts
1	$ 100	$ 100	$ 1,200	$ 1,200	$ 360	$ 360
2	150	250	0	1,200	0	360
3	100	350	0	1,200	0	360
4	100	450	1,100	2,300	0	360
5	150	600	0	2,300	0	360
6	100	700	100	2,400	0	360
7	300	1,000	0	2,400	0	360
8	100	1,100	100	2,500	0	360
9	100	1,200	0	2,500	0	360
10	500	1,700	0	2,500	0	360
11	100	1,800	0	2,500	0	360
12	100	1,900	1,400	3,900	420	780
13	350	2,250	1,550	5,450	465	1,245
14	100	2,350	0	5,450	0	1,245
15	1,500	3,850	0	5,450	0	1,245
16	100	3,950	0	5,450	0	1,245
17	3,500	7,450	7,700	13,150	2,310	3,555
18	100	7,550	0	13,150	0	3,555
19	9,000	16,550	1,150	14,300	0	3,555
20	100	16,650	0	14,300	0	3,555
21	500	17,150	2,280	16,580	684	4,239
22	100	17,250	0	16,580	0	4,239
23	400	17,650	0	16,580	0	4,239
24	1,000	18,650	0	16,580	0	4,239
25	$ 1,500	$ 20,150	$ 2,700	$ 19,280	$ 810	$ 5,049

In this example, the 25 total wagers were made at a total cost of US$20,150 (i.e., the cumulative total of all wagers made), which generated total jackpots of US$19,280 and U.S. withholding tax of US$5,049. The "per session" method used by *Sang Park* in order to determine the "income, gains or profits" from that session, would yield a loss of (US$870). This loss is measured by the difference between the total amount of Jackpots won during that session (i.e., US$19,280), reduced by the total amounts wagered in that session (i.e., US$20,150). The difference is an "in the red" or "negative" number of (US$870), reflecting the economic loss incurred by the non-resident casual gambler.

In this case, we will assume the non-resident gambler started with US$7,000 in his pocket and therefore after the gambling session left the Casino or Race Track with US$1,081.

In contrast, the IRS "per spin" or "per play" method would yield a total amount of "income, gains and profit" of an amount that cannot be determined. The IRS' *non-sequitur* method does not allow the taxpayer a method by which to determine his or her "income, gains and profit". The method simply withholds 30% on jackpots of at least $1,200. In this case, the non-resident gambler has total jackpots of US$19,280. However, the IRS only counts the jackpots of at least US$1,200, which in this case amounts to a total of US$16,830. The IRS "per bet" or "per spin" method, does not allow the taxpayer to even count as his or her tax basis, the amounts of the wagers.

The oddness of this approach by the IRS (i.e., the *non-sequitur*) is only exacerbated, when by all accounts; this gambler had a loss for the session played of (US$870); i.e., total jackpots of US$19,280 reduced by the total amounts wagered in that session of US$20,150.

Worse yet, for this non-resident casual gambler, he started the gambling session with US$7,000 in his pocket and left the Casino with only US$1,081, due to the $5,049 taxes withheld. If the IRS was correct in their determination, he somehow had "income, gains and profit." No common sense reading of the statute or law would conclude that he had "income, gains and profit" and hence, this gambler should be able to bring an action against the IRS to recover all of the US$5,049 withholding tax paid over to the IRS directly by the Casino.

The IRS' non-sequitur method does not allow the taxpayer a method by which to determine his or her "income, gains and profit". The method simply withholds 30% on jackpots of at least $1,200.

In this first session, the non-resident recreational gambler had a loss.

Let's look at another gambling session of 25 wagers that looks quite similar, but which generates total cumulative jackpots of US$36,280 with the same number of cumulative amounts wagered in that session of US$20,150.

Wager Number	Wagered Amounts	Cumulative Wagered Amounts	Jackpot Amounts	Cumulative Jackpot Amounts	Withholding Tax Amounts	Cumulative Withholding Tax Amounts
1	$ 100	$ 100	$ 1,200	$ 1,200	$ 360	$ 360
2	150	250	0	1,200	0	360
3	100	350	0	1,200	0	360
4	100	450	3,100	4,300	930	1,290
5	150	600	0	4,300	0	1,290
6	100	700	100	4,400	0	1,290
7	300	1,000	0	4,400	0	1,290
8	100	1,100	100	4,500	0	1,290
9	100	1,200	0	4,500	0	1,290
10	500	1,700	0	4,500	0	1,290
11	100	1,800	0	4,500	0	1,290
12	100	1,900	3,400	7,900	1,020	2,310
13	350	2,250	1,550	9,450	465	2,775
14	100	2,350	0	9,450	0	2,775
15	1,500	3,850	0	9,450	0	2,775
16	100	3,950	0	9,450	0	2,775
17	3,500	7,450	700	10,150	0	2,775
18	100	7,550	0	10,150	0	2,775
19	9,000	16,550	21,150	31,300	6,345	9,120
20	100	16,650	0	31,300	0	9,120
21	500	17,150	2,280	33,580	684	9,804
22	100	17,250	0	33,580	0	9,804
23	400	17,650	0	33,580	0	9,804
24	1,000	18,650	0	33,580	0	9,804
25	$ 1,500	$ 20,150	$ 2,700	$ 36,280	$ 810	$ 10,614

At first, it seems clear that this recreational gambler has "income, gains or profit" determined by the cumulative jackpots of US$36,280 with the same number of cumulative amounts wagered in that session of US$20,150.

This "income, gains or profit" would therefore be the total amount of Jackpots won during that session (i.e., US$36,280), reduced by the total amounts wagered in that session (i.e., US$20,150). The difference "in the black", would presumably be "income, gains or profit"; i.e., **US$16,310**. This is indeed the correct result per the Court in *Sang Park*. The determination of tax is 30%

against this amount of **US$16,310**, which yields a total U.S. income tax owing of **US$4,839** (not $10,614).

Incidentally, this gambler started with US$10,000 in his pocket and will be leaving the Casino with US$15,516 (which is increased by the jackpots won and decreased by the 30% withholding tax on all jackpots of at least US$1,200). This cash flow analysis is reflected below:

Starting Cash in Pocket ($10,000): Running Total of Amounts in Pocket	Wagered Amounts (Single Wagers)	Jackpot Amounts (Single Jackpots)	Withholding Tax Amounts	Funds Increased-(Decreased) in Pocket	Cumulative Funds Increased-(Decreased) in Pocket
$ 10,000	$ (100)	$ 1,200	$ (360)	$ 740	$ 740
$ 10,740	$ (150)	$ -	$ -	$ (150)	$ 590
$ 10,590	$ (100)	$ -	$ -	$ (100)	$ 490
$ 10,490	$ (100)	$ 3,100	$ (930)	$ 2,070	$ 2,560
$ 12,560	$ (150)	$ -	$ -	$ (150)	$ 2,410
$ 12,410	$ (100)	$ 100	$ -	$ -	$ 2,410
$ 12,410	$ (300)	$ -	$ -	$ (300)	$ 2,110
$ 12,110	$ (100)	$ 100	$ -	$ -	$ 2,110
$ 12,110	$ (100)	$ -	$ -	$ (100)	$ 2,010
$ 12,010	$ (500)	$ -	$ -	$ (500)	$ 1,510
$ 11,510	$ (100)	$ -	$ -	$ (100)	$ 1,410
$ 11,410	$ (100)	$ 3,400	$ (1,020)	$ 2,280	$ 3,690
$ 13,690	$ (350)	$ 1,550	$ (465)	$ 735	$ 4,425
$ 14,425	$ (100)	$ -	$ -	$ (100)	$ 4,325
$ 14,325	$ (1,500)	$ -	$ -	$ (1,500)	$ 2,825
$ 12,825	$ (100)	$ -	$ -	$ (100)	$ 2,725
$ 12,725	$ (3,500)	$ 700	$ -	$ (2,800)	$ (75)
$ 9,925	$ (100)	$ -	$ -	$ (100)	$ (175)
$ 9,825	$ (9,000)	$ 21,150	$ (6,345)	$ 5,805	$ 5,630
$ 15,630	$ (100)	$ -	$ -	$ (100)	$ 5,530
$ 15,530	$ (500)	$ 2,280	$ (684)	$ 1,096	$ 6,626
$ 16,626	$ (100)	$ -	$ -	$ (100)	$ 6,526
$ 16,526	$ (400)	$ -	$ -	$ (400)	$ 6,126
$ 16,126	$ (1,000)	$ -	$ -	$ (1,000)	$ 5,126
$ 15,126	$ (1,500)	$ 2,700	$ (810)	$ 390	$ 5,516
$ 15,516					

Not surprisingly, the IRS "per spin" or "per play" method would yield a total amount of "income, gains and profit" of an amount that again cannot be determined. The IRS method simply withholds 30% on jackpots of at least $1,200. In this case, the non-resident gambler has total jackpots of US$36,280. However, the IRS only counts the jackpots of at least US$1,200, which in this case amounts to a total of US$35,380. Again, the IRS "per bet" or "per spin" method, does not allow the taxpayer to count as his or her tax basis, the amounts of the wagers. The IRS approach would mean that total withholding taxes of **US$10,614** is the amount owing by the non-resident gambler.

This represents an important difference, since the amount of taxes owing is more than double!! That is, of **US$10,614** per the IRS yet only **US$4,839** per the law as articulated by the Court in *Sang Park*. In this case, the casual gambler should be able to bring a refund action against the IRS for the difference of excess tax withheld of **$5,775** (i.e., **US$10,614** withheld less **US$4,839** actual tax owing).

E. Tax Election by Non-Resident Gambler

Fortunately, for you, there may be a legal method by which you can obtain the same tax results as a resident recreational gambler; i.e., and deduct your losses in the fashion explained above for resident gamblers. If you meet the residency requirements of days present in the United States, you can make an election to be taxed as a "resident" of the U.S. You must have been physically present in the U.S. for at least 31 days in the calendar year you want to make the election (and satisfy additional requirements of the statute).

> **Fortunately, if you are a non-resident casual gambler, there may be a legal method by which you can obtain the same tax results as a resident recreational gambler; i.e., and deduct your losses in the fashion explained above.**

However, you need to be aware, that such election means you will be subject to U.S. income taxation on your worldwide income. It also means you have various U.S. information reporting requirements regarding your foreign assets. If you have little income separate from your gambling activities (i.e., worldwide) and have few or non-complicated foreign assets (e.g., shares of non-U.S. private companies, non-U.S. bank and financial accounts, foreign trusts, etc.), this election to be taxed as a resident may well be advisable for you.

F. Factors Used by Courts and in Treasury Regulations to Determine "for Profit" Activity

Now you understand the important difference between a casual or recreational gambler compared to one who engages in a trade or business of gambling. It is clear; there are important tax benefits to the latter for non-resident gamblers. However, the really BIG question is; how does one really make the distinction between the two types of gamblers? Which one are you?

There are numerous court cases in the U.S. that have addressed when a gambler is merely a casual gambler or engaged in a trade or business. The courts have found it is a determination to be resolved on the basis of all the facts and circumstances of a particular case.

The Treasury published regulations that set forth nine (9) factors that are normally to be considered when determining whether a taxpayer is engaged in an activity "for profit." The courts have used these factors routinely determining when gambling at slot machines or other gambling such as betting at the Race Track, is an activity that gives rise to a trade or business.

- **Factor 1: The manner in which the taxpayer carries on the activity.** Does the gambler conduct the gambling activities in a professional and businesslike manner? Does the gambler maintain complete and accurate books and records? If the answer to the above is yes, this factor lends itself towards a finding of gambling as a profit motive. This factor is worth emphasizing, since accounting records and thorough bookkeeping of all gambling transactions is important to help demonstrate the

> **This factor is worth overemphasizing, since accounting records and thorough bookkeeping of all gambling transactions is important to help demonstrate the gambler undertakes the gambling activity in a businesslike manner.**

gambler undertakes the gambling activity in a businesslike manner.

- **Factor 2: The expertise of the taxpayer or his advisors.** If the gambler undertakes extensive study of the gambling industry, strategies and play methods, this may indicate the gambler has the expertise necessary. This factor also includes the experts hired by the gambler to advise and educate the gambler (e.g., business consultants, gambling experts, lawyers and accountants). The Courts have found that experienced advisors who are engaged to assist the gambler in the undertaking; helps demonstrate a profit motive of the gambler.
- **Factor 3: The time and effort expended by the taxpayer in carrying on the activity.** A gambler who devotes much time and effort to engaging in gambling activities will usually be considered to have an intention to make a profit. The Courts have held that a gambler can have full time jobs and still undertake gambling as a business. The more time devoted to gambling, the better. Devoting more time to gambling compared to any other business undertaking will help support this factor in any particular analysis.
- **Factor 5: The success of the taxpayer in carrying on other similar or dissimilar activities.** A taxpayer's success in converting non-gambling activities from unprofitable to profitable enterprises may indicate a profit motive for gambling. This factor is always difficult to apply in the context of gamblers, since it is usually very difficult to logically link other business or employment undertakings with gambling, as the skill sets are often quite different.
- **Factor 6: The taxpayer's history of income or losses with respect to the gambling activity.** A history of being profitable, without having consistent years of losses, can help demonstrate the gambling activity was undertaken for profit, and hence is a trade or business of the non-resident gambler.

- **Factor 7: The amount of occasional profits, if any, which are earned from gambling.** Even a few occasional and large wins, can help demonstrate that a gambler has undertaken the activity for profit and hence it is part of a trade or business.

> **Even a few occasional and large wins, can help demonstrate that a gambler has undertaken the activity for profit and hence it is part of a trade or business.**

- **Factor 8: The financial status of the taxpayer.** If the gambler has large amounts of income from other sources, this is a factor that may indicate he or she does not undertake gambling as a for-profit business enterprise. This, like all of the factors, is just one factor that is to be analyzed pursuant to the regulations.

- **Factor 9: Elements of personal pleasure or recreation from gambling.** Gambling at a Casino or playing bets at a Race Track is commonly understood to be a form of entertainment and activity undertaken for pleasure. An exclusive or near exclusive focus on gambling as a business undertaking, without a routine of going to Las Vegas or Atlantic City or any other alluring place, to go to shows, go shopping or otherwise take vacation type detours, will help demonstrate this factor in favor of the gambler.

CHAPTER 8
CASINO "COMPS"

Casinos regularly provide their customers, particularly their best customers with so-called "comps" or complimentary goods and services in return for gambling at their Casino. Typical "comps" provided include food and beverage items from the Casino restaurants. "Comps" also commonly include hotel stays at no charge for the gambler and sometimes additional rooms for friends of family members of the gambler. It is also fairly common for "high roller" customers to get tickets to shows, concerts, sporting events such as boxing and other recreational activities found in and around the Casino.

"Comps" also commonly include hotel stays at no charge for the gambler and sometimes additional rooms for friends of family members of the gambler. It is also fairly common for "high roller" customers to get tickets to shows, concerts, sporting events such as boxing and other recreational activities found in and around the Casino.

Casinos have a method by which they carefully track who is gambling how much. The amount of "comps" that can be provided by any given Casino is based largely upon the amount of gambling activity (the amount of "play"); the more the gambling the greater the "comps". The most sophisticated Casinos use complex formulas and methods for determining the exact amount of "comps" to be provided.

A. How Casinos Track Comps

Casinos principally use the "player's card" to track the amount and volume of gambling of any particular gambler to help them determine the amount of "comps" provided (if any) to any particular gambler.

B. What is the U.S. Tax Treatment?

In the case of trade or business gamblers, the U.S. Tax Court has held that comps obtained in connection with a gambling business are considered income for purposes of tax reporting. The analysis used by the Tax Court was that the income activity was sufficiently related to the gambling loss activity. Since recreational non-resident gamblers, do not get to calculate losses (per IRC Section 165(d)), it is doubtful that the U.S. Tax Court's analysis in *Libutti v. Commissioner*[19], below, should be extended beyond U.S. trade or business gamblers:

> ***The relationship between petitioner's comps and his wagering is close, direct, evident, and strong. The comps are sufficiently related to his gambling losses for purposes of section 165(d). We hold that petitioner's comps are 'gains from * * * [wagering] transactions' under section 165(d).***

In the case of trade or business gamblers, the U.S. Tax Court above has held that comps obtained in connection with a gambling business are indeed to be considered income for purposes of tax reporting. The analysis used by the Tax Court was that the income activity was sufficiently related to the gambling loss activity rule.[20] However, since recreational non-resident gamblers are not able to calculate losses (per IRC Section 165(d)), it is doubtful that the U.S. Tax Court's analysis in *Libutti v. Commissioner*[21], above, should be extended beyond U.S. trade or business gamblers.

It is an open question as to whether recreational gamblers need to include "comps" into their items of income. However, if you are in a trade or business as a gambler you do indeed need to include the amount of "comps" received from your gambling activities as income.

---

[19] T.C. Memo. 1996-108.

[20] See, IRC Section 165(d).

[21] T.C. Memo. 1996-108.

CHAPTER 9
U.S. INCOME TAX TREATIES – WHAT YOU NEED TO KNOW TO ESCAPE THE "ECONOMIC MADNESS" OF HOW THE IRS ADMINISTERS THE 30% WITHHOLDING TAX

The next topic might sound terribly thrilling or terribly boring to you, depending upon your tastes and the country where you reside. No matter which side you fall on, the topic of Income Tax Treaties can be very important to you, depending upon which country around the world is your home. Income tax treaties are a form of international law negotiated between the U.S. federal government and different governments around the world. Some of these income tax treaties ("Tax Treaties"), but not all, have specific provisions in them pertaining to gambling and gaming activities.

A. Income Tax Treaties

For those non-U.S. citizens who reside in one of the following countries, there may be specific international tax law relief available to you under an income tax treaty for your winnings from U.S. Casinos and Race Tracks:

- Austria
- Belgium
- Bulgaria
- *Canada (the special case)
- Czech Republic
- Denmark
- Finland
- France
- Germany
- Hungary
- Iceland
- Ireland
- Italy
- Japan
- Latvia
- Lithuania
- Luxembourg
- Malta
- Netherlands
- Russia
- Slovak Republic
- Slovenia
- South Africa
- Spain
- Sweden
- Tunisia
- Turkey
- Ukraine
- United Kingdom

If you are a tax resident in one of the above countries, you can probably avoid in its entirety the *non-sequitur* of the IRS explained above (with Canada being the special case). The misfortune that befell our gambler who made two wagers and then paid a U.S. "infinite" income tax rate can be avoided from inception and in its entirety if an applicable income tax treaty applies.

The following income tax treaties with European countries, Turkey and Russia exempt gambling gains from being subject to U.S. withholding tax by virtue of an income tax treaty with these countries (there are 25 treaties), provided procedural requirements are satisfied.

Austria: Article 21 – Other Income;

Belgium: Article 20 – Other Income;

Bulgaria: Article 20 – Other Income;

Czech Republic: Article 22 – Other Income;

Denmark: Article 21 – Other Income;

Finland: Article 21 – Other Income;
France: Article 22 – Other Income;
Germany: Article 21 – Other Income;
Hungary: Article 19 – Other Income;
Iceland: Article 20 – Other Income;
Ireland: Article 22 – Other Income
Italy: Article 22 – Other Income;
Latvia: Article 22 – Other Income;
Lithuania: Article 22 – Other Income;
Luxembourg: Article 22 – Other Income;
Netherlands: Article 23 – Other Income;
Russian Federation: Article 19 – Other Income;
Slovak Republic: Article 22 – Other Income;
Slovenia: Article 21 – Other Income;
Spain: Article 23 – Other Income
Sweden: Article 22 – Other Income;
Turkey: Article 21 – Other Income;
Ukraine: Article 21 – Other Income;
United Kingdom: Article 22 – Other Income;
EXCEPTION: Malta: Article 21 – Other Income – Gambling income of residents of Malta is taxed at 10%

Unfortunately, nothing is ever simple when discussing U.S. income tax and tax concepts. Just because you live or have a home in one of these several countries, does not mean you automatically avoid the U.S. 30% withholding tax on your Casino earnings. Indeed, there a number of requirements that you will need to satisfy.

i. Tax Treaty Interpretation for Gamblers

You also need to be certain the applicable treaty in your case exempts gambling income from taxation. The treaty analysis can be confusing, since the words "gambling", "gambler", "gambling income," "wagers" or "gambling loss" or the like may never appear in the text of the relevant income tax treaty. Indeed, the U.S.-Japan Income Tax Treaty (2003) has no express reference to gambling or gambling income. Nowhere in the treaty is gambling activities directly addressed. Fortunately, the U.S. commentary to the U.S.-Japan Income Tax Treaty provides that Article 21 ("Other Income") explains that "items of income covered by Article 21 include income from **gambling**". Article 21 says that unless otherwise addressed in the treaty, the country where the individual is resident (e.g., in this example a Japanese resident of Japan) is the only country that can impose taxation on the income (e.g., Japan in this case). This means, that gamblers from Japan, who earn income at U.S. Race Tracks or Casinos are not subject to U.S. income taxation on that U.S. source wagering income; provided you "jump through all the hoops" described below.

You might have hit the "proverbial" jackpot if you reside in one of the following countries and can comply with the various procedural provisions under the law (including having a U.S. "ITIN") and the applicable income tax treaty:

Austria	**Lithuania**
Belgium	**Luxembourg**
Bulgaria	**Malta**
Czech Republic	**Netherlands**
Denmark	**Russia**
Finland	**Slovak Republic**
France	**Slovenia**
Germany	**South Africa**
Hungary	**Spain**
Iceland	**Sweden**
Ireland	**Tunisia**
Italy	**Turkey**
Japan	**Ukraine**
Latvia	**United Kingdom**

As explained below, the procedural requirements to get the U.S. Race Tracks or Casinos not to withhold on such Japanese resident gambler must be satisfied; e.g., including an ITIN, etc.

The U.S.-Japanese Income Tax Treaty regarding "Other Income" is in sharp contrast with other U.S. income tax treaties (e.g., with Mexico), which provides the opposite rule. This opposite rule, says that unless the treaty addresses some form of income, the country where the income arises, may impose taxation on such income.[22] In the case of U.S. Race Tracks or Casinos, the income will always arise in the U.S. and hence the U.S. may always impose U.S. income taxation on such wagering income.

The U.S.-Canada income tax treaty has a special disposition regarding taxation of gambling gains and income. Canadian residents may claim gambling losses, but only to the extent of gambling income. They must file a claim for refund, after the fact, of federal income tax withheld.

---

22 See, Article 23 of the U.S.-Mexico Income Tax Treaty, for instance, which provides in its entirety as follows:

> Items of income of a resident of a Contracting State [e.g., Mexico] not dealt with in the foregoing Articles of this Convention and arising in the other Contracting State [e.g., the U.S.] may be taxed in that other State [e.g., the U.S.].

The U.S.- Mexico income tax treaty has no exemption.

ii. Special Canadian Rule

Canada has a special rule under the United States - Canadian income tax treaty. Canadian resident gamblers have a separate set of procedural requirements they must follow to more easily recover tax refunds. Article XXII of the United States - Canada Income Tax Treaty sets forth this special rule that specifically provides that losses incurred in gambling and wagering transactions can be offset and deducted to the same extent that losses would be deductible if they were incurred by a resident of the United States.

This means that a Canadian gambler gets to account for their recreational gambling in the same manner that a United States resident recreational gambler can. Therefore, Canadians can reduce their wagering losses against wagering jackpots when they file a US tax return. Canadians, however, cannot avoid the 30% withholding in its entirety from inception.

B. Procedural Requirements – Tax Treaties

It is always worth trying to see if a non-resident gambler qualifies for income tax treaty benefits. There are three principle procedural requirements that must be satisfied by the non-resident gambler to avoid the 30% withholding tax in its entirety.

i. Bona Fide Tax Residency

First, the non-resident gambler must qualify as a resident under the applicable income tax treaty. This is not always easy, since each income tax treaty has specific provisions that must be complied with. For instance, the U.K. treaty defines a resident of the U.K. as " . . any person who, under the laws of [the UK] . . . is liable to tax therein by reason of his domicile, residence, citizenship, place of management, place of incorporation, or any other criterion of a similar nature. This term, however, does not include any person who is liable to tax in that State in respect only of income from sources in [the UK] . . . or of profits attributable to a permanent establishment in [the UK] . . ." This is a fairly typical definition of who is a resident under most provisions of the income tax treaties with the United States.

ii. Certification of Residency – Under Penalty of Perjury

The second requirement is related with the first requirement and obligates the non-U.S. citizen to certify, under penalty of perjury, that his or her tax residency is indeed in that other country. This certification is prepared and must be filed using IRS Form W-8BEN, a complete copy of which can be found below.

None of the income tax treaties in force with South American countries, in fact only Venezuela has an income tax treaty with the U.S., exempt U.S. gambling gains and income from withholding tax. Hence all gamblers resident in South America are subject to the 30% statutory rate.

This IRS Form W-8BEN requires the gambler to provide their address and residency in their home country (e.g., Austria, Belgium, Bulgaria, Canada, Czech Republic, Denmark, Finland, France, Germany, Hungary, Iceland, Ireland, Italy, Japan, Latvia, Lithuania, Luxembourg, Malta, Netherlands, Russia, Slovak Republic, Slovenia, South Africa, Spain, Sweden, Tunisia, Turkey, Ukraine, or the United Kingdom). The address information is completed in Part I, shown below:

None of the income tax treaties in force with countries in the Oceania region (there are only two; Australia and New Zealand) exempt U.S. gambling gains and income from withholding tax (30%).

Form **W-8BEN**
(Rev. February 2006)
Department of the Treasury
Internal Revenue Service

Certificate of Foreign Status of Beneficial Owner for United States Tax Withholding

▶ Section references are to the Internal Revenue Code. ▶ See separate instructions.
▶ Give this form to the withholding agent or payer. Do not send to the IRS.

OMB No. 1545-1621

Do not use this form for:	Instead, use Form:
• A U.S. citizen or other U.S. person, including a resident alien individual	W-9
• A person claiming that income is effectively connected with the conduct of a trade or business in the United States	W-8ECI
• A foreign partnership, a foreign simple trust, or a foreign grantor trust (see instructions for exceptions)	W-8ECI or W-8IMY
• A foreign government, international organization, foreign central bank of issue, foreign tax-exempt organization, foreign private foundation, or government of a U.S. possession that received effectively connected income or that is claiming the applicability of section(s) 115(2), 501(c), 892, 895, or 1443(b) (see instructions)	W-8ECI or W-8EXP

Note: *These entities should use Form W-8BEN if they are claiming treaty benefits or are providing the form only to claim they are a foreign person exempt from backup withholding.*

• A person acting as an intermediary	W-8IMY

Note: *See instructions for additional exceptions.*

Part I Identification of Beneficial Owner (See instructions.)

1 Name of individual or organization that is the beneficial owner

2 Country of incorporation or organization

3 Type of beneficial owner: ☐ Individual ☐ Corporation ☐ Disregarded entity ☐ Partnership ☐ Simple trust ☐ Grantor trust ☐ Complex trust ☐ Estate ☐ Government ☐ International organization ☐ Central bank of issue ☐ Tax-exempt organization ☐ Private foundation

4 Permanent residence address (street, apt. or suite no., or rural route). **Do not use a P.O. box or in-care-of address.**

City or town, state or province. Include postal code where appropriate. | Country (do not abbreviate)

5 Mailing address (if different from above)

City or town, state or province. Include postal code where appropriate. | Country (do not abbreviate)

6 U.S. taxpayer identification number, if required (see instructions) ITIN needed here ☐ SSN or ITIN ☐ EIN

7 Foreign tax identifying number, if any (optional)

8 Reference number(s) (see instructions)

The next part of the form that must be completed is Part II, which requires the tax treaty information is shown below:

Part II **Claim of Tax Treaty Benefits** (if applicable)

9 **I certify that (check all that apply):**

a ☐ The beneficial owner is a resident of .... within the meaning of the income tax treaty between the United States and that country.

b ☐ If required, the U.S. taxpayer identification number is stated on line 6 (see instructions).

c ☐ The beneficial owner is not an individual, derives the item (or items) of income for which the treaty benefits are claimed, and, if applicable, meets the requirements of the treaty provision dealing with limitation on benefits (see instructions).

d ☐ The beneficial owner is not an individual, is claiming treaty benefits for dividends received from a foreign corporation or interest from a U.S. trade or business of a foreign corporation, and meets qualified resident status (see instructions).

e ☐ The beneficial owner is related to the person obligated to pay the income within the meaning of section 267(b) or 707(b), and will file Form 8833 if the amount subject to withholding received during a calendar year exceeds, in the aggregate, $500,000.

10 **Special rates and conditions** (if applicable—see instructions): The beneficial owner is claiming the provisions of Article .... of the treaty identified on line 9a above to claim a .... % rate of withholding on (specify type of income): ....

Explain the reasons the beneficial owner meets the terms of the treaty article: ....

....

Part III **Notional Principal Contracts**

11 ☐ I have provided or will provide a statement that identifies those notional principal contracts from which the income is **not** effectively connected with the conduct of a trade or business in the United States. I agree to update this statement as required.

Part IV **Certification**

Under penalties of perjury, I declare that I have examined the information on this form and to the best of my knowledge and belief it is true, correct, and complete. I further certify under penalties of perjury that:

1 I am the beneficial owner (or am authorized to sign for the beneficial owner) of all the income to which this form relates,

2 The beneficial owner is not a U.S. person,

3 The income to which this form relates is (a) not effectively connected with the conduct of a trade or business in the United States, (b) effectively connected but is not subject to tax under an income tax treaty, or (c) the partner's share of a partnership's effectively connected income, **and**

4 For broker transactions or barter exchanges, the beneficial owner is an exempt foreign person as defined in the instructions.

Furthermore, I authorize this form to be provided to any withholding agent that has control, receipt, or custody of the income of which I am the beneficial owner or any withholding agent that can disburse or make payments of the income of which I am the beneficial owner.

Sign Here ▶ .... Signature of beneficial owner (or individual authorized to sign for beneficial owner) | .... Date (MM-DD-YYYY) | .... Capacity in which acting

For Paperwork Reduction Act Notice, see separate instructions. Cat. No. 25047Z Form **W-8BEN** (Rev. 2-2006)

Printed on Recycled Paper

Although all of the above steps might seem somewhat complicated, they are the simple ones.

There is no withholding tax on gambling gains not subject to U.S. withholding tax by virtue of an income tax treaty with these countries in the African continent (there are only 2 countries) South Africa: Article 21 – Other Income; Tunisia: Article 21 – Other Income.

iii. U.S. Individual Taxpayer Identification Number ("ITIN") – the "Catch 22"

The last procedural requirement is for the gambler to obtain a U.S. Individual Taxpayer Identification Number commonly referred to as an "ITIN". This is wherein lies a so-called "Catch 22" from the book of the same title. You probably do not have, and would have no reason to have an ITIN. A "Catch 22" is when the steps required cannot be satisfied because of another requirement, which is unable to be satisfied because of another requirement. It sends the person around in circles. That is the case with non-residents and U.S. ITINs.

The U.S. has no income tax treaties in force with Central America countries and hence U.S. gambling gains are not exempt from withholding. The 30% statutory rate applies.

The non-resident gambler will most certainly get frustrated with the steps and requirements of obtaining an ITIN. An entire book could be written explaining ITINs, how they are obtained and why the IRS (largely due to Congressional hearings) and cases of fraud makes it very difficult to obtain an ITIN. The first step is the completion of IRS Form W-7, a complete copy of which can be found below.

Form **W-7**
(Rev. January 2012)
Department of the Treasury
Internal Revenue Service

Application for IRS Individual Taxpayer Identification Number

► For use by individuals who are not U.S. citizens or permanent residents.
► See instructions.

OMB No. 1545-0074

FOR IRS USE ONLY

An IRS individual taxpayer identification number (ITIN) is for federal tax purposes only.

Before you begin:

- ***Do not submit*** *this form if you have, or are eligible to get, a U.S. social security number (SSN).*
- *Getting an ITIN does not change your immigration status or your right to work in the United States and does not make you eligible for the earned income credit.*

Reason you are submitting Form W-7. Read the instructions for the box you check. **Caution:** If you check box **b, c, d, e, f, or g, you must file a tax return with Form W-7 unless you meet one of the exceptions** (see instructions).

a ☒ Nonresident alien required to get ITIN to claim tax treaty benefit
b ☐ Nonresident alien filing a U.S. tax return
c ☐ U.S. resident alien **(based on days present in the United States)** filing a U.S. tax return
d ☐ Dependent of U.S. citizen/resident alien
e ☐ Spouse of U.S. citizen/resident alien
Enter name and SSN/ITIN of U.S. citizen/resident alien (see instructions) ►
f ☐ Nonresident alien student, professor, or researcher filing a U.S. tax return or claiming an exception
g ☐ Dependent/spouse of a nonresident alien holding a U.S. visa
h ☐ Other (see instructions) ►
Additional information for a and f: Enter treaty country ► Country and treaty article number ► Treaty Provision

Name (see instructions)	1a First name	Middle name	Last name
Name at birth if different ►	1b First name	Middle name	Last name
Applicant's mailing address	2 Street address, apartment number, or rural route number. **If you have a P.O. box, see separate instructions.**		
	City or town, state or province, and country. Include ZIP code or postal code where appropriate.		
Foreign (non-U.S.) address (if different from above) (see instructions)	3 Street address, apartment number, or rural route number. **Do not use a P.O. box number.**		
	City or town, state or province, and country. Include ZIP code or postal code where appropriate.		
Birth information	4 Date of birth (month / day / year)	Country of birth	City and state or province (optional) — 5 ☐ Male ☐ Female
Other information	6a Country(ies) of citizenship	6b Foreign tax I.D. number (if any)	6c Type of U.S. visa (if any), number, and expiration date

6d Identification document(s) submitted (see instructions) ☒ Passport ☐ Driver's license/State I.D. ☐ USCIS documentation ☐ Other

Who is willing to provide their original passport from their home country to the United States Internal Revenue Service?

Issued by: No.: Exp. date: / / Date of entry into the United States (MM/DD/YYYY) / /

6e Have you previously received a U.S. temporary taxpayer identification number (TIN) or employer identification number (EIN)?
☐ **No/Do not know.** Skip line 6f.
☐ **Yes.** Complete line 6f. If more than one, list on a sheet and attach to this form (see instructions).

6f Enter: TIN or EIN ► and
Name under which it was issued ►

6g Name of college/university or company (see instructions)
City and state Length of stay

Sign Here

Under penalties of perjury, I (applicant/delegate/acceptance agent) declare that I have examined this application, including accompanying documentation and statements, and to the best of my knowledge and belief, it is true, correct, and complete. I authorize the IRS to disclose to my acceptance agent returns or return information necessary to resolve matters regarding the assignment of my IRS individual taxpayer identification number (ITIN), including any previously assigned taxpayer identifying number.

Signature of applicant (if delegate, see instructions) | Date (month / day / year) / / | Phone number

Keep a copy for your records.

Name of delegate, if applicable (type or print) | Delegate's relationship to applicant ► ☐ Parent ☐ Court-appointed guardian ☐ Power of Attorney

Acceptance Agent's Use ONLY

Signature | Date (month / day / year) / / | Phone | Fax

Name and title (type or print) | Name of company | EIN | Office Code

For Paperwork Reduction Act Notice, see separate instructions. Cat. No. 10229L Form **W-7** (Rev. 1-2012)

Completing and filling out the Form W-7 is not the difficult part.

To reiterate, the difficult part is how the IRS requires an ITIN to be obtained. In short, the best approach to obtain an ITIN and file IRS Form W-7, is to submit ***your original passport*** to the IRS along with the properly completed IRS Form W-7. Yes, this is not a typo, ***your original passport*** is requested by the IRS to approve the W-7 and issue an ITIN. Who wants to send your original passport to another foreign government's tax authority? There are other original documents that can be submitted. Also, it commonly takes 6-18 weeks for the IRS to process the form and issue an ITIN, or even longer, if they reject the initial application which is common. Who has 6-18 weeks of time to wait for an ITIN from the IRS; especially if the application is filed while you are physically in the United States on your gambling trip?

Who has 6-18 weeks of time to wait for an ITIN from the IRS; especially if the application is filed while you are physically in the United States on your gambling trip??

Some Casinos and Race Tracks have experts who can explain and assist you in obtaining an ITIN through the proper filing of IRS Form W-7. Fortunately, some Casinos and Race Tracks are even so-called "Acceptance Agents" with the IRS and can help facilitate in obtaining an ITIN so that your original document (e.g., your passport of your home country) does not have to be submitted directly to the IRS. This Acceptance Agents process is a simplified procedure by which original documents, such as your passport, can be provided to the qualifying representative of the Casino or Race Track (instead of the IRS) who can then receive and review the original documents and then file directly with the IRS, Form W-7, to obtain your ITIN. You get to keep your original document, e.g., passport in such cases.

Who wants to send your original passport to another foreign government's tax agency authority?

Most importantly, without an ITIN, you will not be able to get the treaty benefits of reducing the 30% withholding tax to 0% (or 10% in the case of Malta tax residents). If you are entitled to tax treaty benefits, because you live in a tax treaty country, you will clearly want to obtain an ITIN so the Casinos and Race Tracks will NOT withhold the 30% on the gross jackpots or winnings in amounts of US$1,200 or more.

There is only one income tax treaty in Asia which eliminates the U.S. withholding tax on gambling gains not subject to U.S. withholding tax by virtue of an income tax treaty in Asia. Japan: Article 21 – Other Income

The difficult part is being willing to provide and submit your original passport from your home country directly to the Internal Revenue Service when the application is filed for the ITIN. Worse, it will typically take multiple weeks before the IRS even issues the ITIN to you. In the meantime, the Internal Revenue Service has your original passport in their possession which will mean you cannot travel internationally, including too or from the United States. Although, there are alternative original documents, that you can submit, instead of your passport, the Internal Revenue Service increasingly rejects these applications filed. Therein lies the proverbial "Catch 22."

Also, you can obtain a certified copy of your passport from your own government (with Apostille certification) that can be submitted with your W-7. You can have your government issue you the certified copy of your passport in your home country, or request your Consulate's office in the United States to issue such an Apostille certification of your passport. You can then submit this Apostille certification along with your original IRS Form W-7.

Incidentally, the tax treaties do not provide specific procedural requirements that have to be fulfilled in order to claim treaty benefits.[23]

This OECD explanation does not address directly the exact type of procedural requirements that can be imposed by a country when claiming treaty benefits. Notwithstanding, it clearly explains the notion that the requirements imposed by a country should be

---

23 Notwithstanding, when addressing some procedural aspects for the limits on source taxation, the OECD commentaries establish:

"... the Convention does not settle procedural questions and each State is free to use the procedure provided in its domestic law in order to apply the limits provided by the Convention. A state can therefore automatically limit the tax that it levies in accordance with the relevant provisions of the Convention, subject to possible prior verification of treaty entitlement, or it can impose the tax provided for under its domestic law and subsequently refund the part of that tax that exceeds the amount that it can levy under the provision of the Convention. As a general rule, in order to ensure expeditious implementation of taxpayers' benefits under a treaty, the first approach is the highly preferable method. If a refund system is needed, it should be based on observable difficulties in identifying entitlement to treaty benefits. Also, where the second approach is adopted, it is extremely important that the refund be made expeditiously, especially if no interest is paid on the amount of the refund, as any undue delay in making that refund is a direct cost to the taxpayer." See, Paragraph 26.2 of the Commentaries on Article 1 of the OECD Model.

reasonable, in order to ensure that the taxpayer is entitled to the treaty benefits. The IRS will surely conclude the IRS Form W-7 with original documents requirements such as your passport is a "reasonable" procedural requirement.

As a practical matter, you should consider obtaining an ITIN prior to gambling in the U.S., if you live in a country with an income tax treaty that reduces, or eliminates the 30% withholding tax from gambling winnings. Ideally, you will succesfully file IRS Form W-7, submitting the documents required under the IRS rules, and apply for an ITIN prior to ever making a long distance trip to the U.S. Casinos or Race Tracks. The IRS website publishes those Casinos who are registered as acceptance agents on their website. There are only a few http://www.irs.gov/Individuals/Acceptance-Agent-Program

CHAPTER 10
HOW TO BE PREPARED TO GO UP AGAINST GOLIATH

This last chapter may well be the most important chapter in the book. Up until now, you have hopefully received a fairly good understanding of what can be a terribly complicated topic. The purpose of this final chapter is to explain the key concepts you need to know so you can recover money, the United States withholding taxes, that you are legally due under the law. It is not a simple process since "the House" (the IRS) has the edge. To the extent you are more knowledgeable and more informed; you can reduce this "House edge."

A. Knowing How to Report Your Gambling Activities

As explained in the chapter regarding accounting for your gambling activities, there is probably nothing in your control of greater importance. You need to have clear records of all gambling, how much invested/at risk, how much won, how much was lost and the details among those three points. These records need to be kept up-to-date and as contemporaneous as possible with each gambling session of wagering activity.

Now that you have a good overview of these rules, sometimes very complicated rules, the next steps is putting all of this together, to develop a good plan to report and operate your gambling activities. The following flowchart provides a basic summary of the main steps that need to be taken to be prepared to protect your legal rights for income taxes withheld arising from your gambling activities:

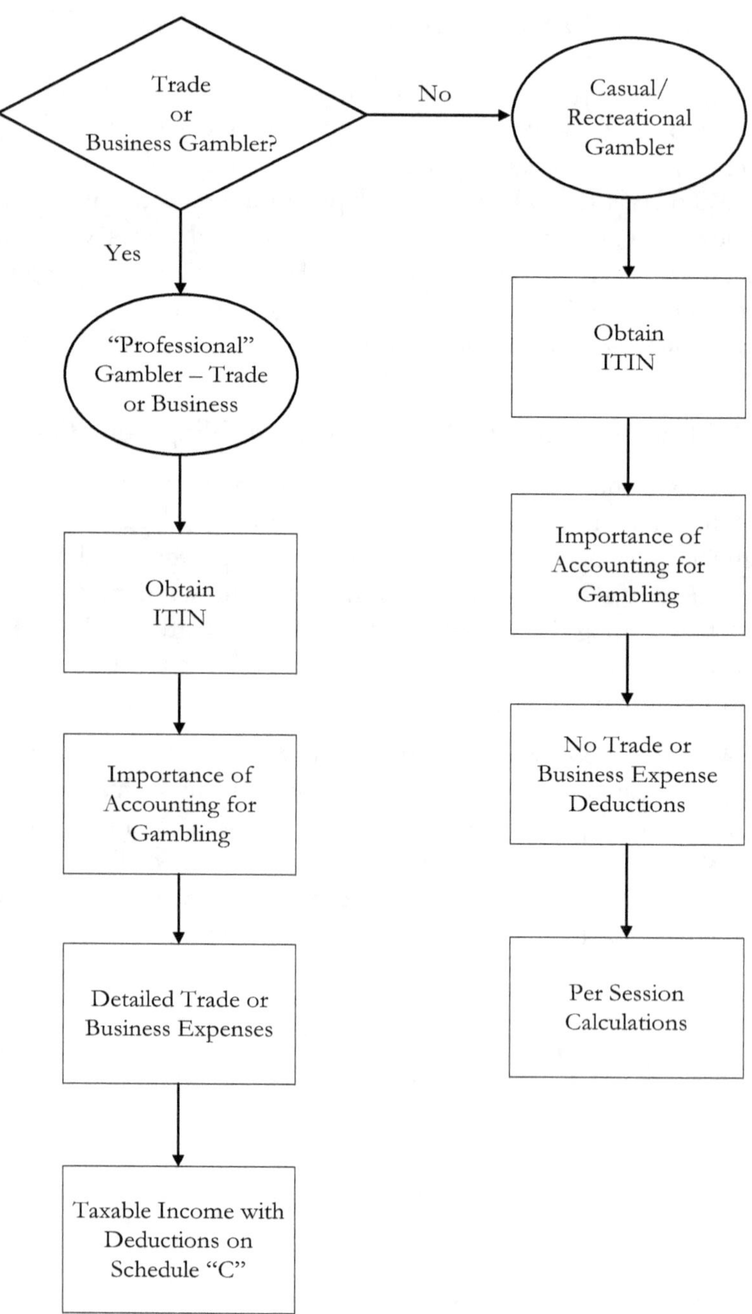
Trade
or
Business Gambler?
No
Casual/
Recreational
Gambler
Yes
"Professional"
Gambler – Trade
or Business
Obtain
ITIN
Importance of
Accounting for
Gambling
Detailed Trade or
Business Expenses
Taxable Income with
Deductions on
Schedule "C"
Obtain
ITIN
Importance of
Accounting for
Gambling
No Trade or
Business Expense
Deductions
Per Session
Calculations

The key items you will want to make sure you address are the following:

- Determine whether you are in the "trade or business" of gambling?
- Develop and maintain a detailed accounting system to track your gambling activity.
- File for, and obtain your ITIN.
- Be aware of the key time limits in the U.S. tax law that imposes specific limitations over your rights vis-à-vis the IRS.
- Keep good records to be used in the event of IRS audits and suits for tax refunds you might need to make against the IRS in the U.S. District Court or U.S. Court of Federal Claims.

B. IRS Audits

This book has focused on being able to let you be prepared so that you can win at the game of tax refunds as a non-resident gambler. If you've been following these rules and are well-prepared, you'll be prepared when the Internal Revenue Service commences an audit to determine whether or not your records regarding your gambling activities will withstand their scrutiny. In short, if your records and information are complete and accurate, you will prevail against the Internal Revenue Service.

Next, you need to be prepared for an audit to be undertaken by the Internal Revenue Service. They typically refuse to refund taxes (the 30%) from gambling activities of non-residents. Their current approach is to simply assume all non-resident gamblers are not entitled to any refund of taxes. While this statement may be a bit of an exaggeration, you need to be prepared for and assume the worst. The professional experience of this author is that this is exactly the approach taken by the Internal Revenue Service with non-resident gamblers. In the defense of the

Plus, there is no real downside to the Internal Revenue Service if they simply hold onto your taxes and not provide you a refund.

Internal Revenue Service, they have been critiqued by the Inspector General and will take great care not to provide refunds if they think they cannot be fully supported under the law. Plus, there is no real downside to the Internal Revenue Service if they simply hold onto your taxes and not provide you a refund. The IRS wins if you do not bring a legal action, in the form of a suit, for refund of taxes. This approach leaves the non-resident gambler, in the lurch; with no realistic expectation of recovery of taxes. Therefore you need to be extraordinarily detailed and well prepared and well advised on the steps you need to take.

i. No Time Limits Imposed on the IRS

The law does not require the Internal Revenue Service to commence an audit during any given time for the gambling activities of a non-resident, if certain safeguards are not taken by the taxpayer. In other words, if you do not take the safeguards, the Internal Revenue Service can audit you four or five, or more years in the past. For this reason, it is important that you take the safeguards, so that the three-year statute of limitations will be imposed against the Internal Revenue Service. This way, they will not be able to audit you for many years in the past. Their audits will have to be limited to the most recent three years.

ii. Defending Against an IRS Audit

Probably the easiest step you can take is to have a good international tax lawyer familiar with the special rules on non-resident gamblers represent you to handle and deal directly with the Internal Revenue Service. That way, you do not have to communicate directly or provide documents or information directly to the Internal Revenue Service. Your representative can handle all of those steps on your behalf.

Remember, you as a non-resident gambler have the burden of proof to show that your calculations and your records are complete and accurate. You have the burden of proving that your calculation method is consistent with the law. You also have to be prepared, that the Internal Revenue Service will take a position wholly unsupported by the law as articulated by the court in *Sang Park*, that the taxes owed will be far more than the amounts you calculate for a non-resident gambler. The IRS will likely hold on to your money.

This result will almost necessarily mean you will have to defend your position against the Internal Revenue Service. You should therefore have an idea of the process and what you will be up against.

C. IRS Administrative Appeals

There is an administrative procedure by which a gambler will need to file directly with the Internal Revenue Service, prior to bringing a suit for a refund in the courts. The details of the administrative appeals process are beyond the scope of this book and chapter; however it is important to note that there are specific requirements that must be satisfied by you as a non-resident gambler directly with the Internal Revenue Service. Again, it is probably much easier for you to have a good international tax lawyer familiar with the special rules on non-resident gamblers represent you during this Internal Revenue Service administrative appeals process to handle and deal directly with the Internal Revenue Service. That way, you do not have to communicate directly or provide documents or information directly to the Internal Revenue Service. Your representative can handle all of those steps on your behalf.

Paying a success fee, based upon the amount recovered from the IRS will not make you incur any "out-of-pocket" costs or expenses.

It is important that you get this work done cost efficiently on your behalf, as different tax advisors charge using wildly different methods by which they represent their clients. Ideally, you will find someone expert in this United States international tax world for non-resident gamblers who simply will charge you based upon the success and results obtained. Instead of charging you for their time and work, irrespective of the success or lack of success they might have. Paying a success fee, based upon the amount recovered from the IRS will not make you incur any "out-of-pocket" costs or expenses.

In short, all challenges of the law by taxpayers, including non-resident gamblers, need to be first addressed before the administrative appeals process of the Internal Revenue Service. You will be required to file a so-called protest letter with appeals. You have a right to do this directly or through a legal representative, such as an experienced U.S. international tax lawyer. An experienced US international tax lawyer can represent you as your agent before the Internal Revenue Service. You will need to have the attorney authorized through a special power of attorney, Internal Revenue Service Form 2848. You or your representative, such as an experienced U.S. international tax lawyer can request a formal meeting with the Internal Revenue Service appeals officer. It is important you or your representative understands well what legal requirements you have, particularly regarding statements and documents provided.

United States law and tax law in the most extreme of cases can impose criminal liability against a non-resident gambler who provides false information or false documents. You also need to be prepared that the appeals officer will likely rule in favor of the government and against you as the non-resident gambler, simply because of the method by which they calculate United States withholding tax due.

i. Preparing Your Case for Administrative Appeals

You will need to be able to provide detailed and comprehensive information regarding all accountings of your gambling activities. It is important that your records are complete and help you carry your burden of proof. You will need to have copies of all Internal Revenue Service Forms 1042s, "coin-in" and "coin-out"; all jackpots and winnings and all amounts invested in your daily gambling activities, including loans or "markers" you might have obtained. There is a specific process that you need to follow to substantiate, authenticate and then be able to provide such books and records to the Internal Revenue Service appeals officer.

D. U.S. Tax Court – Limited Jurisdiction

Next, we will assume your case will now need to go to Court; as is true for most of these non-resident gambler cases. This is true because the Internal Revenue Service typically rejects these claims for tax refund. Accordingly, you'll need to decide which court in the United States has jurisdiction over your case. It is doubtful that the United States Tax Court will have jurisdiction, since the Internal Revenue Service would first have to issue a tax assessment against you.

E. Suits for Tax Refund

If you cannot go to the United States Tax Court to get your tax refunds back, where can you go? Where is your legal remedy under United States tax law? Hopefully, the IRS will refund your taxes; your money. This is unlikely, because as explained above, the Internal Revenue Service has every incentive to simply sit and wait indefinitely and not refund your money.

i. U.S. Court of Federal Claims

The Court of Federal claims is probably the venue where you will need to file your suit for a refund, since the Jurisdiction of this court is typical for tax refund cases when persons have their domicile outside the United States. The Court of Federal Claims does not provide a jury trial and is based in Washington DC.

ii. U.S. District Court – Limited Jurisdiction

It may be possible that you file a suit for refund against the government in the United States District Court. You will probably have a right to a jury trial in United States District Court. However, there are strict limits regarding domicile and jurisdiction with the United States District Court since you are a non-resident gambler and therefore probably reside outside of United States on a regular ongoing basis.

F. Proper Representation

Hire an international tax lawyer with experience in these specific types of cases. Ask for references. The tax law and process is fraught with complexity. Hire someone reputable.

G. Statutes of Limitations – Don't Lose on Your Taxes

If you cannot file a suit for refund within the time limitations imposed under the law, you will lose your suit for refund and your money. The United States law has strict time limits imposed under what is called the "statute of limitations," and restricts the ability to recover taxes owed against the government if those time frames are not respected and the legal requirements satisfied timely.

i. Three-Year Statute of Limitations

In many cases, but not necessarily all cases, there is a three-year statute of limitations. This three-year time frame is crucial in determining exactly when that time expires. This book does not attempt to try to explain the technical details of the three-year statute of limitations, but importantly highlights that it exists and that if you cannot satisfy the legal requirements in the law within that timeframe, you will not be able to recover taxes withheld and paid by the Casinos or Race Track directly to the Internal Revenue Service. If you cannot satisfy these criteria, your suit for refund of taxes withheld against the United States federal government will fail. You will lose your money.

ii. Two-Year Statute of Limitations

Finally, there is also a two-year statute of limitations in the statute. It is important generally to be aware that this imposes a shorter timeframe, when it is applicable. Whether the two-year statute of limitations or three years statute of limitations applies in your particular case, you need to be aware that you cannot delay in pursuing your case against United States federal government for tax refund suits in court.

Do not lose your rights to recover your money from the IRS (U.S. Treasury) that is rightfully yours.

Conclusion

If you have a solid plan, you can come out a winner and recover your taxes legally owed to you by the U.S. Treasury Department. You need to understand the basics of the law and always keep good records. Although learning these rules and following them may be tedious, it will mean real money in your pocket. You will be glad that you now have the insight to understand that for **Non-U.S. Citizen Gamblers - It's All in the Taxes!**

Appendix

a. IRS Form – 1042 (http://www.irs.gov/pub/irs-pdf/f1042.pdf)

Form **1042**
Department of the Treasury
Internal Revenue Service

Annual Withholding Tax Return for U.S. Source Income of Foreign Persons

▶ Information about Form 1042 and its separate instructions is at *www.irs.gov/form1042.*

OMB No. 1545-0096

2012

If this is an amended return, check here . . . . . ▶ ☐

Name of withholding agent	Employer identification number	For IRS Use Only	
		CC	FD
Number, street, and room or suite no. (if a P.O. box, see instructions)		RD	FF
		CAF	FP
City or town, province or state, and country (including postal code)		CR	I
		EDC	SIC

If you will not be liable for returns in the future, check here ▶ ☐ Enter date final income paid ▶

Check if you are a: QI/Withholding foreign partnership or trust ☐ NQI/Flow-through entity ☐ (See instructions.)

Record of Federal Tax Liability (Do not show federal tax deposits here.)

Line No.	Period ending	Tax liability for period (including any taxes assumed on Form(s) 1000)	Line No.	Period ending	Tax liability for period (including any taxes assumed on Form(s) 1000)	Line No.	Period ending	Tax liability for period (including any taxes assumed on Form(s) 1000)
1	Jan. 7		21	May 7		41	Sept. 7	
2	15		22	15		42	15	
3	22		23	22		43	22	
4	31		24	31		44	30	
5	Jan. total		25	May total		45	Sept. total	
6	Feb. 7		26	June 7		46	Oct. 7	
7	15		27	15		47	15	
8	22		28	22		48	22	
9	29		29	30		49	31	
10	Feb. total		30	June total		50	Oct. total	
11	Mar. 7		31	July 7		51	Nov. 7	
12	15		32	15		52	15	
13	22		33	22		53	22	
14	31		34	31		54	30	
15	Mar. total		35	July total		55	Nov. total	
16	Apr. 7		36	Aug. 7		56	Dec. 7	
17	15		37	15		57	15	
18	22		38	22		58	22	
19	30		39	31		59	31	
20	Apr. total		40	Aug. total		60	Dec. total	

61 **No. of Forms 1042-S filed: a** On paper **b** Electronically

62 **For all Form(s) 1042-S and 1000: a** Gross income paid **b** Taxes withheld or assumed

63a Total tax liability (add monthly total lines from above) . . . **63a**

b Adjustments (see instructions) **63b**

c Total **net tax** liability (combine lines 63a and 63b) . . . . ▶ **63c**

64 Total paid by electronic funds transfer (or with a request for an extension of time to file) for 2012 . . . . . **64**

65 Enter overpayment applied as a credit from 2011 Form 1042 . **65**

66 Credit for amounts withheld by other withholding agents (see instructions) **66**

67 **Total payments.** Add lines 64 through 66 . . . . ▶ **67**

68 If line 63c is larger than line 67, enter **balance due** here . . . **68**

69 If line 67 is larger than line 63c, enter **overpayment** here . . . **69**

70 Apply overpayment on line 69 to (check one): ☐ **Credit on 2013 Form 1042** or ☐ **Refund**

71 Excise tax on specified federal procurement payments included on line 63a. (Total payments made x 2% =) **71**

Third Party Designee — Do you want to allow another person to discuss this return with the IRS (see instructions)? ☐ Yes. Complete the following. ☐ No
Designee's name ▶ Phone no. ▶ Personal identification number (PIN) ▶

Sign Here — Under penalties of perjury, I declare that I have examined this return, including accompanying schedules and statements, and to the best of my knowledge and belief, it is true, correct, and complete. Declaration of preparer (other than withholding agent) is based on all information of which preparer has any knowledge.
Your signature ▶ Date Capacity in which acting ▶
Daytime phone number ▶

Paid Preparer Use Only — Print/Type preparer's name | Preparer's signature | Date | Check ☐ if self-employed | PTIN
Firm's name ▶ Firm's EIN ▶
Firm's address ▶ Phone no.

For Privacy Act and Paperwork Reduction Act Notice, see instructions. Cat. No. 11384V Form **1042** (2012)

b. IRS Form – 1042-S (http://www.irs.gov/pub/irs-pdf/f1042s_12.pdf)

Form **1042-S** Department of the Treasury Internal Revenue Service

Foreign Person's U.S. Source Income Subject to Withholding **2012**

☐ **AMENDED** ☐ **PRO-RATA BASIS REPORTING**

OMB No. 1545-0096

Copy A for Internal Revenue Service

1 Income code	2 Gross income	3 Withholding allowances	4 Net income	5 Tax rate / 6 Exemption code	7 Federal tax withheld / 8 Withholding by other agents / 9 Total withholding credit

10 Amount repaid to recipient	14 Recipient's U.S. TIN, if any ▶ ☐ SSN or ITIN ☐ EIN ☐ QI-EIN
11 Withholding agent's EIN ▶ ☐ EIN ☐ QI-EIN	15 Recipient's foreign tax identifying number, if any / 16 Country code
12a WITHHOLDING AGENT'S name	17 NQI's/FLOW-THROUGH ENTITY'S name / 18 Country code
12b Address (number and street)	19a NQI's/Entity's address (number and street)
12c Additional address line (room or suite no.)	19b Additional address line (room or suite no.)
12d City or town, province or state, country, ZIP or foreign postal code	19c City or town, province or state, country, ZIP or foreign postal code
13a RECIPIENT'S name / 13b Recipient code	20 NQI's/Entity's U.S. TIN, if any ▶
13c Address (number and street)	21 PAYER'S name and TIN (if different from withholding agent's)
13d Additional address line (room or suite no.)	22 Recipient account number (optional)
13e City or town, province or state, country, ZIP or foreign postal code	23 State income tax withheld / 24 Payer's state tax no. / 25 Name of state

For Privacy Act and Paperwork Reduction Act Notice, see instructions. Cat. No. 11386R Form **1042-S** (2012)

c. IRS Form – W-2G (only applicable for U.S. resident gamblers) (http://www.irs.gov/pub/irs-pdf/fw2g.pdf)

3232 ☐ VOID ☐ CORRECTED

PAYER'S name, street address, city or town, province or state, country, ZIP or foreign postal code	1 Gross winnings $	2 Date won	OMB No. 1545-0238 **2013** **Form W-2G**
	3 Type of wager	4 Federal income tax withheld $	
	5 Transaction	6 Race	**Certain Gambling Winnings**
	7 Winnings from identical wagers $	8 Cashier	
Federal identification number Telephone number	9 Winner's taxpayer identification no.	10 Window	For Privacy Act and Paperwork Reduction Act Notice, see the **2013 General Instructions for Certain Information Returns.**
WINNER'S name	11 First I.D.	12 Second I.D.	
Street address (including apt. no.)	13 State/Payer's state identification no.	14 State winnings $	
City or town, province or state, country, and ZIP or foreign postal code	15 State income tax withheld $	16 Local winnings $	**File with Form 1096**
	17 Local income tax withheld $	18 Name of locality	**Copy A** **For Internal Revenue Service Center**

Under penalties of perjury, I declare that, to the best of my knowledge and belief, the name, address, and taxpayer identification number that I have furnished correctly identify me as the recipient of this payment and any payments from identical wagers, and that no other person is entitled to any part of these payments.

Signature ▶ **Date ▶**

Form **W-2G** Cat. No. 10138V www.irs.gov/w2g Department of the Treasury - Internal Revenue Service

Do Not Cut or Separate Forms on This Page – Do Not Cut or Separate Forms on This Page

d. IRS Form – W-8BEN (http://www.irs.gov/pub/irs-pdf/fw8ben.pdf)

Form **W-8BEN**
(Rev. February 2006)
Department of the Treasury
Internal Revenue Service

Certificate of Foreign Status of Beneficial Owner for United States Tax Withholding

▶ Section references are to the Internal Revenue Code. ▶ See separate instructions.
▶ Give this form to the withholding agent or payer. Do not send to the IRS.

OMB No. 1545-1621

Do not use this form for:	**Instead, use Form:**
• A U.S. citizen or other U.S. person, including a resident alien individual	W-9
• A person claiming that income is effectively connected with the conduct of a trade or business in the United States	W-8ECI
• A foreign partnership, a foreign simple trust, or a foreign grantor trust (see instructions for exceptions)	W-8ECI or W-8IMY
• A foreign government, international organization, foreign central bank of issue, foreign tax-exempt organization, foreign private foundation, or government of a U.S. possession that received effectively connected income or that is claiming the applicability of section(s) 115(2), 501(c), 892, 895, or 1443(b) (see instructions)	W-8ECI or W-8EXP
Note: *These entities should use Form W-8BEN if they are claiming treaty benefits or are providing the form only to claim they are a foreign person exempt from backup withholding.*	
• A person acting as an intermediary	W-8IMY

Note: *See instructions for additional exceptions.*

Part I **Identification of Beneficial Owner** (See instructions.)

1 Name of individual or organization that is the beneficial owner

2 Country of incorporation or organization

3 Type of beneficial owner: ☐ Individual ☐ Corporation ☐ Disregarded entity ☐ Partnership ☐ Simple trust ☐ Grantor trust ☐ Complex trust ☐ Estate ☐ Government ☐ International organization ☐ Central bank of issue ☐ Tax-exempt organization ☐ Private foundation

4 Permanent residence address (street, apt. or suite no., or rural route). **Do not use a P.O. box or in-care-of address.**

City or town, state or province. Include postal code where appropriate.

Country (do not abbreviate)

5 Mailing address (if different from above)

City or town, state or province. Include postal code where appropriate.

Country (do not abbreviate)

6 U.S. taxpayer identification number, if required (see instructions) ☐ SSN or ITIN ☐ EIN

7 Foreign tax identifying number, if any (optional)

8 Reference number(s) (see instructions)

Part II **Claim of Tax Treaty Benefits** (if applicable)

9 **I certify that (check all that apply):**

a ☐ The beneficial owner is a resident of .... within the meaning of the income tax treaty between the United States and that country.

b ☐ If required, the U.S. taxpayer identification number is stated on line 6 (see instructions).

c ☐ The beneficial owner is not an individual, derives the item (or items) of income for which the treaty benefits are claimed, and, if applicable, meets the requirements of the treaty provision dealing with limitation on benefits (see instructions).

d ☐ The beneficial owner is not an individual, is claiming treaty benefits for dividends received from a foreign corporation or interest from a U.S. trade or business of a foreign corporation, and meets qualified resident status (see instructions).

e ☐ The beneficial owner is related to the person obligated to pay the income within the meaning of section 267(b) or 707(b), and will file Form 8833 if the amount subject to withholding received during a calendar year exceeds, in the aggregate, $500,000.

10 **Special rates and conditions** (if applicable—see instructions): The beneficial owner is claiming the provisions of Article .... of the treaty identified on line 9a above to claim a .... % rate of withholding on (specify type of income): ....
Explain the reasons the beneficial owner meets the terms of the treaty article: ....

Part III **Notional Principal Contracts**

11 ☐ I have provided or will provide a statement that identifies those notional principal contracts from which the income is **not** effectively connected with the conduct of a trade or business in the United States. I agree to update this statement as required.

Part IV **Certification**

Under penalties of perjury, I declare that I have examined the information on this form and to the best of my knowledge and belief it is true, correct, and complete. I further certify under penalties of perjury that:

1 I am the beneficial owner (or am authorized to sign for the beneficial owner) of all the income to which this form relates,

2 The beneficial owner is not a U.S. person,

3 The income to which this form relates is (a) not effectively connected with the conduct of a trade or business in the United States, (b) effectively connected but is not subject to tax under an income tax treaty, or (c) the partner's share of a partnership's effectively connected income, and

4 For broker transactions or barter exchanges, the beneficial owner is an exempt foreign person as defined in the instructions.

Furthermore, I authorize this form to be provided to any withholding agent that has control, receipt, or custody of the income of which I am the beneficial owner or any withholding agent that can disburse or make payments of the income of which I am the beneficial owner.

Sign Here ▶ .... Signature of beneficial owner (or individual authorized to sign for beneficial owner) .... Date (MM-DD-YYYY) .... Capacity in which acting

For Paperwork Reduction Act Notice, see separate instructions. Cat. No. 25047Z Form **W-8BEN** (Rev. 2-2006)

Printed on Recycled Paper

e. IRS Form – W-7 (http://www.irs.gov/pub/irs-pdf/fw7.pdf)

Form **W-7** (Rev. January 2012) Department of the Treasury Internal Revenue Service

Application for IRS Individual Taxpayer Identification Number

► For use by individuals who are not U.S. citizens or permanent residents.
► See instructions.

OMB No. 1545-0074

FOR IRS USE ONLY

An IRS individual taxpayer identification number (ITIN) is for federal tax purposes only.

Before you begin:

- ***Do not submit*** *this form if you have, or are eligible to get, a U.S. social security number (SSN).*
- *Getting an ITIN does not change your immigration status or your right to work in the United States and does not make you eligible for the earned income credit.*

Reason you are submitting Form W-7. Read the instructions for the box you check. **Caution:** If you check box **b, c, d, e, f,** or **g, you must file a tax return with Form W-7 unless you meet one of the exceptions** (see instructions).

a ☐ Nonresident alien required to get ITIN to claim tax treaty benefit
b ☐ Nonresident alien filing a U.S. tax return
c ☐ U.S. resident alien **(based on days present in the United States)** filing a U.S. tax return
d ☐ Dependent of U.S. citizen/resident alien
e ☐ Spouse of U.S. citizen/resident alien
Enter name and SSN/ITIN of U.S. citizen/resident alien (see instructions) ►
f ☐ Nonresident alien student, professor, or researcher filing a U.S. tax return or claiming an exception
g ☐ Dependent/spouse of a nonresident alien holding a U.S. visa
h ☐ Other (see instructions) ►
Additional information for a and f: Enter treaty country ► and treaty article number ►

Name (see instructions) — **1a** First name | Middle name | Last name

Name at birth if different ► — **1b** First name | Middle name | Last name

Applicant's mailing address — **2** Street address, apartment number, or rural route number. **If you have a P.O. box, see separate instructions.**
City or town, state or province, and country. Include ZIP code or postal code where appropriate.

Foreign (non-U.S.) address (if different from above) (see instructions) — **3** Street address, apartment number, or rural route number. **Do not use a P.O. box number.**
City or town, state or province, and country. Include ZIP code or postal code where appropriate.

Birth information — **4** Date of birth (month / day / year) | Country of birth | City and state or province (optional) | **5** ☐ Male ☐ Female

Other information — **6a** Country(ies) of citizenship | **6b** Foreign tax I.D. number (if any) | **6c** Type of U.S. visa (if any), number, and expiration date

6d Identification document(s) submitted (see instructions) ☐ Passport ☐ Driver's license/State I.D. ☐ USCIS documentation ☐ Other
Issued by: No.: Exp. date: / / Date of entry into the United States (MM/DD/YYYY) / /

6e Have you previously received a U.S. temporary taxpayer identification number (TIN) or employer identification number (EIN)?
☐ **No/Do not know.** Skip line 6f.
☐ **Yes.** Complete line 6f. If more than one, list on a sheet and attach to this form (see instructions).

6f Enter: TIN or EIN ► and Name under which it was issued ►

6g Name of college/university or company (see instructions)
City and state Length of stay

Sign Here

Under penalties of perjury, I (applicant/delegate/acceptance agent) declare that I have examined this application, including accompanying documentation and statements, and to the best of my knowledge and belief, it is true, correct, and complete. I authorize the IRS to disclose to my acceptance agent returns or return information necessary to resolve matters regarding the assignment of my IRS individual taxpayer identification number (ITIN), including any previously assigned taxpayer identifying number.

► Signature of applicant (if delegate, see instructions) | Date (month / day / year) / / | Phone number

Keep a copy for your records.

► Name of delegate, if applicable (type or print) | Delegate's relationship to applicant ► ☐ Parent ☐ Court-appointed guardian ☐ Power of Attorney

Acceptance Agent's Use ONLY

► Signature | Date (month / day / year) / / | Phone | Fax
► Name and title (type or print) | Name of company | EIN | Office Code

For Paperwork Reduction Act Notice, see separate instructions. Cat. No. 10229L Form **W-7** (Rev. 1-2012)

f. IRS Form – W-9 (only applicable for U.S. resident gamblers (http://www.irs.gov/pub/irs-pdf/fw9.pdf)

Form **W-9**
(Rev. December 2011)
Department of the Treasury
Internal Revenue Service

Request for Taxpayer Identification Number and Certification

Give Form to the requester. Do not send to the IRS.

Print or type
See Specific Instructions on page 2.

Name (as shown on your income tax return)

Business name/disregarded entity name, if different from above

Check appropriate box for federal tax classification:
☐ Individual/sole proprietor ☐ C Corporation ☐ S Corporation ☐ Partnership ☐ Trust/estate

☐ Limited liability company. Enter the tax classification (C=C corporation, S=S corporation, P=partnership) ▶

☐ Exempt payee

☐ Other (see instructions) ▶

Address (number, street, and apt. or suite no.)

Requester's name and address (optional)

City, state, and ZIP code

List account number(s) here (optional)

Part I **Taxpayer Identification Number (TIN)**

Enter your TIN in the appropriate box. The TIN provided must match the name given on the "Name" line to avoid backup withholding. For individuals, this is your social security number (SSN). However, for a resident alien, sole proprietor, or disregarded entity, see the Part I instructions on page 3. For other entities, it is your employer identification number (EIN). If you do not have a number, see *How to get a TIN* on page 3.

Note. If the account is in more than one name, see the chart on page 4 for guidelines on whose number to enter.

Social security number

☐☐☐ – ☐☐ – ☐☐☐☐

Employer identification number

☐☐ – ☐☐☐☐☐☐☐

Part II **Certification**

Under penalties of perjury, I certify that:

1. The number shown on this form is my correct taxpayer identification number (or I am waiting for a number to be issued to me), and
2. I am not subject to backup withholding because: (a) I am exempt from backup withholding, or (b) I have not been notified by the Internal Revenue Service (IRS) that I am subject to backup withholding as a result of a failure to report all interest or dividends, or (c) the IRS has notified me that I am no longer subject to backup withholding, and
3. I am a U.S. citizen or other U.S. person (defined below).

Certification instructions. You must cross out item 2 above if you have been notified by the IRS that you are currently subject to backup withholding because you have failed to report all interest and dividends on your tax return. For real estate transactions, item 2 does not apply. For mortgage interest paid, acquisition or abandonment of secured property, cancellation of debt, contributions to an individual retirement arrangement (IRA), and generally, payments other than interest and dividends, you are not required to sign the certification, but you must provide your correct TIN. See the instructions on page 4.

Sign Here **Signature of U.S. person** ▶ **Date** ▶

General Instructions

Section references are to the Internal Revenue Code unless otherwise noted.

Purpose of Form

A person who is required to file an information return with the IRS must obtain your correct taxpayer identification number (TIN) to report, for example, income paid to you, real estate transactions, mortgage interest you paid, acquisition or abandonment of secured property, cancellation of debt, or contributions you made to an IRA.

Use Form W-9 only if you are a U.S. person (including a resident alien), to provide your correct TIN to the person requesting it (the requester) and, when applicable, to:

1. Certify that the TIN you are giving is correct (or you are waiting for a number to be issued),

2. Certify that you are not subject to backup withholding, or

3. Claim exemption from backup withholding if you are a U.S. exempt payee. If applicable, you are also certifying that as a U.S. person, your allocable share of any partnership income from a U.S. trade or business is not subject to the withholding tax on foreign partners' share of effectively connected income.

Note. If a requester gives you a form other than Form W-9 to request your TIN, you must use the requester's form if it is substantially similar to this Form W-9.

Definition of a U.S. person. For federal tax purposes, you are considered a U.S. person if you are:

• An individual who is a U.S. citizen or U.S. resident alien,

• A partnership, corporation, company, or association created or organized in the United States or under the laws of the United States,

• An estate (other than a foreign estate), or

• A domestic trust (as defined in Regulations section 301.7701-7).

Special rules for partnerships. Partnerships that conduct a trade or business in the United States are generally required to pay a withholding tax on any foreign partners' share of income from such business. Further, in certain cases where a Form W-9 has not been received, a partnership is required to presume that a partner is a foreign person, and pay the withholding tax. Therefore, if you are a U.S. person that is a partner in a partnership conducting a trade or business in the United States, provide Form W-9 to the partnership to establish your U.S. status and avoid withholding on your share of partnership income.

Cat. No. 10231X Form **W-9** (Rev. 12-2011)

g. IRS Form - 2848 (http://www.irs.gov/pub/irs-pdf/f2848.pdf)

Form **2848**
(Rev. March 2012)
Department of the Treasury
Internal Revenue Service

Power of Attorney and Declaration of Representative

▶ Type or print. ▶ See the separate instructions.

OMB No. 1545-0150
For IRS Use Only
Received by:
Name
Telephone
Function
Date / /

Part I **Power of Attorney**

Caution: *A separate Form 2848 should be completed for each taxpayer. Form 2848 will not be honored for any purpose other than representation before the IRS.*

1 Taxpayer information. Taxpayer must sign and date this form on page 2, line 7.

Taxpayer name and address	Taxpayer identification number(s)	
	Daytime telephone number	Plan number (if applicable)

hereby appoints the following representative(s) as attorney(s)-in-fact:

2 Representative(s) must sign and date this form on page 2, Part II.

Name and address	CAF No. PTIN Telephone No. Fax No.
Check if to be sent notices and communications ☐	Check if new: Address ☐ Telephone No. ☐ Fax No. ☐
Name and address	CAF No. PTIN Telephone No. Fax No.
Check if to be sent notices and communications ☐	Check if new: Address ☐ Telephone No. ☐ Fax No. ☐
Name and address	CAF No. PTIN Telephone No. Fax No.
	Check if new: Address ☐ Telephone No. ☐ Fax No. ☐

to represent the taxpayer before the Internal Revenue Service for the following matters:

3 Matters

Description of Matter (Income, Employment, Payroll, Excise, Estate, Gift, Whistleblower, Practitioner Discipline, PLR, FOIA, Civil Penalty, etc.) (see instructions for line 3)	Tax Form Number (1040, 941, 720, etc.) (if applicable)	Year(s) or Period(s) (if applicable) (see instructions for line 3)

4 Specific use not recorded on Centralized Authorization File (CAF). If the power of attorney is for a specific use not recorded on CAF, check this box. See the instructions for Line 4. **Specific Uses Not Recorded on CAF** ▶ ☐

5 Acts authorized. Unless otherwise provided below, the representatives generally are authorized to receive and inspect confidential tax information and to perform any and all acts that I can perform with respect to the tax matters described on line 3, for example, the authority to sign any agreements, consents, or other documents. The representative(s), however, is (are) not authorized to receive or negotiate any amounts paid to the client in connection with this representation (including refunds by either electronic means or paper checks). Additionally, unless the appropriate box(es) below are checked, the representative(s) is (are) not authorized to execute a request for disclosure of tax returns or return information to a third party, substitute another representative or add additional representatives, or sign certain tax returns.

☐ Disclosure to third parties; ☐ Substitute or add representative(s); ☐ Signing a return;

☐ Other acts authorized:

(see instructions for more information)

Exceptions. An unenrolled return preparer cannot sign any document for a taxpayer and may only represent taxpayers in limited situations. An enrolled actuary may only represent taxpayers to the extent provided in section 10.3(d) of Treasury Department Circular No. 230 (Circular 230). An enrolled retirement plan agent may only represent taxpayers to the extent provided in section 10.3(e) of Circular 230. A registered tax return preparer may only represent taxpayers to the extent provided in section 10.3(f) of Circular 230. See the line 5 instructions for restrictions on tax matters partners. In most cases, the student practitioner's (level k) authority is limited (for example, they may only practice under the supervision of another practitioner).

List any specific deletions to the acts otherwise authorized in this power of attorney:

For Privacy Act and Paperwork Reduction Act Notice, see the instructions. Cat. No. 11980J Form **2848** (Rev. 3-2012)

6 **Retention/revocation of prior power(s) of attorney.** The filing of this power of attorney automatically revokes all earlier power(s) of attorney on file with the Internal Revenue Service for the same matters and years or periods covered by this document. If you **do not** want to revoke a prior power of attorney, check here . . . ▶ ☐

YOU MUST ATTACH A COPY OF ANY POWER OF ATTORNEY YOU WANT TO REMAIN IN EFFECT.

7 **Signature of taxpayer.** If a tax matter concerns a year in which a joint return was filed, the husband and wife must each file a separate power of attorney even if the same representative(s) is (are) being appointed. If signed by a corporate officer, partner, guardian, tax matters partner, executor, receiver, administrator, or trustee on behalf of the taxpayer, I certify that I have the authority to execute this form on behalf of the taxpayer.

▶ IF NOT SIGNED AND DATED, THIS POWER OF ATTORNEY WILL BE RETURNED TO THE TAXPAYER.

Signature	Date	Title (if applicable)
Print Name	PIN Number ☐☐☐☐☐	Print name of taxpayer from line 1 if other than individual

Part II Declaration of Representative

Under penalties of perjury, I declare that:

- I am not currently under suspension or disbarment from practice before the Internal Revenue Service;
- I am aware of regulations contained in Circular 230 (31 CFR, Part 10), as amended, concerning practice before the Internal Revenue Service;
- I am authorized to represent the taxpayer identified in Part I for the matter(s) specified there; and
- I am one of the following:

a Attorney—a member in good standing of the bar of the highest court of the jurisdiction shown below.

b Certified Public Accountant—duly qualified to practice as a certified public accountant in the jurisdiction shown below.

c Enrolled Agent—enrolled as an agent under the requirements of Circular 230.

d Officer—a bona fide officer of the taxpayer's organization.

e Full-Time Employee—a full-time employee of the taxpayer.

f Family Member—a member of the taxpayer's immediate family (for example, spouse, parent, child, grandparent, grandchild, step-parent, step-child, brother, or sister).

g Enrolled Actuary—enrolled as an actuary by the Joint Board for the Enrollment of Actuaries under 29 U.S.C. 1242 (the authority to practice before the Internal Revenue Service is limited by section 10.3(d) of Circular 230).

h Unenrolled Return Preparer—Your authority to practice before the Internal Revenue Service is limited. You must have been eligible to sign the return under examination and have signed the return. **See Notice 2011-6 and Special rules for registered tax return preparers and unenrolled return preparers in the instructions.**

i Registered Tax Return Preparer—registered as a tax return preparer under the requirements of section 10.4 of Circular 230. Your authority to practice before the Internal Revenue Service is limited. You must have been eligible to sign the return under examination and have signed the return. **See Notice 2011-6 and Special rules for registered tax return preparers and unenrolled return preparers in the instructions.**

k Student Attorney or CPA—receives permission to practice before the IRS by virtue of his/her status as a law, business, or accounting student working in LITC or STCP under section 10.7(d) of Circular 230. See instructions for Part II for additional information and requirements.

r Enrolled Retirement Plan Agent—enrolled as a retirement plan agent under the requirements of Circular 230 (the authority to practice before the Internal Revenue Service is limited by section 10.3(e)).

▶ IF THIS DECLARATION OF REPRESENTATIVE IS NOT SIGNED AND DATED, THE POWER OF ATTORNEY WILL BE RETURNED. REPRESENTATIVES MUST SIGN IN THE ORDER LISTED IN LINE 2 ABOVE. See the instructions for Part II.

Note: For designations d-f, enter your title, position, or relationship to the taxpayer in the "Licensing jurisdiction" column. See the instructions for Part II for more information.

Designation—Insert above letter (a–r)	Licensing jurisdiction (state) or other licensing authority (if applicable)	Bar, license, certification, registration, or enrollment number (if applicable). See instructions for Part II for more information.	Signature	Date

Form **2848** (Rev. 3-2012)

h. United States Income Tax Treaty Summary of Provisions – Relevant to Gamblers

	Country	Tax Treaty Provision	Tax Rate	Year
1	Austria	Article 21 - Other Income	zero	1996
2	Belgium	Article 20 - Other Income	zero	2006
3	Bulgaria	Article 20 - Other Income	zero	2007
4	Canada	Article 22 - Other Income	30%	1980
5	Czech Republic	Article 22 - Other Income	zero	1993
6	Denmark	Article 21 - Other Income	zero	2000
7	Finland	Article 21 - Other Income	zero	1989
8	France	Article 22 - Other Income	zero	1994
9	Germany	Article 21 - Other Income	zero	1989
10	Hungary	Article 19 - Other Income	zero	1979
11	Iceland	Article 20 - Other Income	zero	2007
12	Ireland	Article 22 - Other Income	zero	1997
13	Italy	Article 22 - Other Income	zero	1999
14	Japan	Article 21 - Other Income	zero	2003
15	Lativa	Article 22 - Other Income	zero	1998
16	Lithuania	Article 22 - Other Income	zero	1998
17	Luxembourg	Article 22 - Other Income	zero	1996
18	Malta	Article 21 - Other Income	10%	2008
19	Netherlands	Article 23 - Other Income	zero	1992
20	Russian Federation	Article 19 - Other Income	zero	1992
21	Slovak Republic	Article 22 - Other Income	zero	1993
22	Slovenia	Article 21 - Other Income	zero	1999
23	South Africa	Article 21 - Other Income	zero	1997
24	Spain	Article 23 - Other Income	zero	1990
25	Sweden	Article 22 - Other Income	zero	1994
26	Tunisia	Article 21 - Other Income	zero	1985
27	Turkey	Article 21 - Other Income	zero	1996
28	Ukraine	Article 21 - Other Income	zero	1994
29	United Kingdom	Article 22 - Other Income	zero	2001

Patrick W. Martin

About the Author - Patrick W. Martin is the leader of the Tax Team of the California based law firm, Procopio, Cory Hargreaves & Savitch LLP ("Procopio") http://www.procopio.com/ His practice emphasizes international tax planning, tax defense and litigation and related international law matters. He has received numerous awards from his tax peers, including the V. Judson Klein Award from the Taxation Section of the California State Bar. The Klein award is given annually to a California tax attorney who exemplifies the qualities of the late V. Judson Klein, namely a high level of legal professionalism, personal integrity and a passion for practicing tax law. He also received the distinguished alumni award from the University of San Diego School of Law.

As an international tax lawyer, he represents foreign individuals, multi-national families, companies, international athletes, entertainers, investors, artists, and authors regarding complex U.S. international tax provisions. He helps resolve international tax controversies and has extensive experience in representing non-resident gamblers in tax cases against the Internal Revenue Service. He has achieved an **AV** Preeminent® Peer Review Ratings™ by his peers, the highest rating in legal ability and ethical standards (Martindale-Hubbell®). He is licensed in California, Texas and Washington, D.C. and practices federal tax law throughout North America.

Patrick W. Martin, Esq

Tel. 619.515.3230 patrick.martin@procopio.com